P9-EDS-872

The Great Archaeologists

The Great Archaeologists

Charles Michael Daugherty

Illustrated by Leonard Everett Fisher

THOMAS Y. CROWELL COMPANY

NEW YORK

The author is grateful to Dr. Walter Fairservis, Jr., Research Associate in Anthropology at the American Museum of Natural History, for helpful criticism and guidance in the writing of this book.

Manufactured in the United States of America
by the Vail-Ballou Press, Inc., Binghamton, N.Y.
Library of Congress Catalog Card No. 62-12812
First Printing

To Katherine Warren Thayer

Contents

Introduction

SCIENCE IS accomplishing so many wonders that we are inclined to take it for granted that science can accomplish anything. Today hardly anyone is surprised or gets angry when a new idea challenges old beliefs. The age of enlightenment in which we are living is also an age of complacency.

A hundred years ago it was much the other way around. Widespread scientific thinking was something new. In its light the universe seemed to be radically changing. Or, to be more exact, people's knowledge and understanding of the universe were changing and great changes seldom occur without great struggles.

The new ideas that were being introduced and examined in the mid-nineteenth century seemed both marvelous and shocking. When revolutionary theories concerning the world and its inhabitants contradicted nearly everything that was taught in the home, school, and church, the reactions of the public, and even of old-guard natural philosophers, as it was still customary to call men of science, were usually strong and sometimes violent.

On no subject did the new thinking encounter stronger opposition than on that of man and his origin. In most minds the questions *Where did he come from and when?* and *What had he been doing all that time?* were satisfactorily answered by the theologians. John Usher, a seventeenth-century Irish churchman, figured out from the Mosaic chronology in the Old Testament that it had been something over four thousand years since Adam and Eve were expelled from the Garden of Eden.

The first valid opposition to traditional ideas about the origin of man came from a few of the new scientific thinkers who, examining the world around them with greater objectivity than had their predecessors, found that a long and wonderful story of the ancient past was to be learned from ample evidence lying buried in the ground. This evidence was available to whoever was prepared to dig, search, study, and deduce. In caves, gravel pits, and excavations, both in England and on the Continent, geologists and keen-eyed amateur scientists found ancient human bones, tools, and weapons buried in the same ground with the bones of extinct species of animals. It was apparent to them that the long-dead human beings whose bones they were recovering, and the extinct animals, had lived at the same time. Consequently there could be no doubt that man's existence extended back into remote prehistoric ages.

The proposition was received with derision by the traditionalists, or fundamentalists, as they were called. Even in the face of such specific evidence as the intermingled bones, many scientists and nearly all nonscientists found it impossible to change beliefs which they had held all their lives. They argued that passing of centuries and shifting of earth could have mixed the relics of periods long separated in time. But the evidence continued to increase and the story told by ancient remains locked deep in successive layers of earth and rock was not easily dismissed. Little by little the new concepts in regard to the ancient past gained acceptance.

Knowledge that the existence of the human race extended back much earlier than had previously been thought possible opened a vast field to exploration and study. And if the archaeologists got off to a bad start in the public eye by taking issue with the Biblical account of Adam and Eve, their researches in Egypt and the Middle East were soon to excite tremendous interest by proving that Biblical references to places and events in ancient Egypt, Babylonia, and Assyria were historically factual.

So the study of man's past and his achievements was helped to the status of a science by the study of the earth's structure. Modern archaeology is largely a product of the scientific thinking of the nineteenth century. Before that century, enthusiasts and students of the remains of ancient cultures were generally known as antiquarians. The forerunners of the archaeologist were collectors of paintings and sculpture, admirers of architecture and all the beautiful things produced by people of former ages. The archaeologist was, and still is, related to the historian. Today he is a scientist as well.

The Great Archaeologists

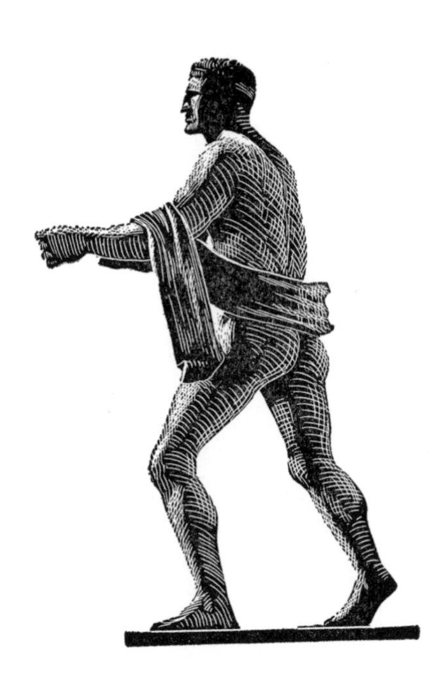

1. The Past Remembered

One sunny spring day five hundred years ago a peasant was plowing a field on an estate not far from Rome when the share struck an obstacle in the ground. "There's a rock down there," he said to himself, "and the sooner I take it out the less trouble it's going to give."

He got a shovel and began to dig. After a few thrusts the shovel scraped the obstacle and revealed a glimpse of its smooth white surface. Removing another spadeful of earth, the man suddenly dropped the shovel and jumped back in horror. The outstretched fingers of a marble hand were reaching at him from the ground. He crossed himself and ran.

As he stumbled across the fields he met the owner of the land, a wealthy nobleman, who was riding over his estate on a tour of inspection. "What's the trouble?" the landowner called. "You look as though you've seen the devil."

"I have, Your Grace. He reached out of the ground and grabbed my ankle."

"I don't believe you. Where did it happen?"

Reluctantly the man led his lord back to the hole. He stood a little distance away while the landowner dismounted and inspected the upthrust hand. After a minute he said, "Go, get three or four others. Bring shovels and ropes. Perhaps we can turn this devil into a god."

Several hours later the diggers had uncovered the marble statue of a naked youth. "It is Apollo himself," their excited master exclaimed. He gave them each a gold coin to ease their consciences for having unearthed a heathen idol. They lifted the statue out of the ground and hauled it by oxcart to the villa, where it was set on a pedestal at the center of the garden.

The lord of the manor was very pleased with his

rare antique statue. Episodes of this nature occurred frequently in the fourteenth and fifteenth centuries. Wealthy people of the time were eager to surround themselves with things of beauty. The revival of learning and creative expression, called the Renaissance, had given new values to intellectual and artistic accomplishments, including those which, in the form of ruins, old inscriptions and manuscripts, painting and sculpture, were relics of ancient times.

Nowhere in Europe was the past more in evidence than in Italy, where once the Greeks had established colonies, the civilization of the Etruscans had flourished, and Rome had superseded both to become the capital of the Western world.

The passing centuries had left the Italian landscape littered with relics of antiquity like a vast unkempt outdoor museum. Some of the architectural remains stood, and still stand, in plain sight where they were originally erected. Others tumbled to the ground. And many, in time, were covered by the earth.

Peasants and workmen who accidently came across ancient remains in the ground were often prevented by ignorance or superstition from preserving what they found—until they learned that there were wealthy men who collected buried fragments of building stone and pieces of pagan sculpture and were willing to pay for them.

During the seventeenth and eighteenth centuries, when science and learning were spreading enlightenment and opening man's consciousness to the infinite wonders of the universe, there were many such collectors. One of the most avid was the king of Naples who, in the 1740s, owned the largest collection of antique statuary in the world. Many of the statues displayed in the royal gardens and museums had come out of the ground at the foot of Mount Vesuvius, where the king's workmen unearthed the lost Roman towns of Herculaneum and Pompeii, buried nearly seventeen centuries before by a violent eruption of the volcano.

It was the first great archaeological discovery. But

the king, instead of proclaiming the news abroad, kept it a secret. Visitors not only were prohibited from the diggings but also were not even welcome to the museum.

One visitor, however, was not only more persistent than others but was also uniquely qualified to appreciate what he managed to see. His name was Johann Joachim Winckelmann. He was born in 1717 in the Prussian village of Stendal, where his father was a shoemaker. As a boy he found escape from the bleakness of poverty in reading. The books he liked best were about distant places and bygone ages. He learned Greek so that he could read the classic authors who lived and wrote hundreds of years before the Christian era. As he grew up, the gods and heroes of the poet Homer became more real to him than the living rulers of his native Prussia, and the European wars of more recent times mattered less than the war between the Greeks and the Trojans as described in the *Iliad*, or the adventures of Ulysses in the *Odyssey*.

If there was any writer he preferred to Homer it was Herodotus, the Greek traveler who visited most of the countries that surrounded the Mediterranean Sea and comprised the civilized world in ancient times. Reading these books, Johann caught such vivid glimpses of the wonders and the beauties of the places described that he dreamed of devoting his life to searching for and admiring what was left of their architecture, sculpture, and painting.

He became the foremost authority of his time on the ancients and their art. In Rome, where he went to live, he so distinguished himself by his learning and his writings that he was appointed chief supervisor of all antiquities in and about the city.

It was in this capacity that he visited Naples to see the diggings at Pompeii and the royal collection. In spite of the secrecy he encountered, he wrote and published a description of the architecture, statuary,

and paintings found in the ground at the foot of Vesuvius. Educated people were eager to hear about lost cities. But what was more important than the entertainment and edification that the report offered the reading public was the precedent it set for a systematic method of collecting and evaluating antiquities. Never before had ancient relics found in the ground been catalogued, described, and made known through publication. It was a procedure which was to become instrumental in turning the pastime of treasure hunting into the scientific investigation of antique ruins and remains.

As an author Winckelmann became best known for

a book entitled *The Art of Antiquity*. His writings and teachings spread his enthusiasm for the achievements of bygone civilizations and put new purpose into the quest for knowledge of man's past. Under his influence other scholars began to understand that the buildings, the art works, and even the remains of humble utilitarian objects left by ancient peoples could add to the historic record and extend it back into unexplored areas of time and place.

Antiquarians turned with renewed interest to the neglected ruins of forgotten civilizations. The most neglected and, as far as could be ascertained, the most ancient ruins known to exist were the massive stone pyramids and columned temples that stood on the banks of the Nile.

2. "The Donkeys" of Napoleon

THROUGHOUT THE SEVENTEENTH and eighteenth centuries France and England, then the two most powerful nations in Europe, vied with one another for world domination. The repercussions of their wars and negotiations were felt far and wide—as far from either country, for instance, as Egypt.

In July, 1798, the young French general, Napoleon Bonaparte, invaded Egypt. His real enemy, of course, was France's long-standing and increasingly powerful rival, England. But he was not yet ready to meet such a formidable opponent face to face. He set out instead to weaken Britain by challenging her claims to empire in the East. If he could win Egypt for France, he reasoned, the victory would be a steppingstone enabling him to conquer India.

Napoleon respected learning, especially the sciences. In addition to the troops, weapons, and supplies necessary to wage war, he included in his expeditionary force a group of more than a hundred civilians who were perhaps the most unwarlike individuals ever to accompany an army into battle. Instead of swords and firearms they carried books and scientific instruments. Their mission was to make a study of the history and the present conditions of the land of the Nile.

Army slang, originating in some long-forgotten joke made by a soldier on the march or around the campfire, nicknamed these scholars and scientists "the donkeys." Their number included some of the most brilliant men in Europe. Among them was an adventurous artist named Dominique Vivant Denon. He was born in 1747 at Chalon-sur-Saône in France and grew up in the environment of luxury which the upper class enjoyed during the reign of Louis XV. As befitted a gentleman of the period, he was endowed with a variety of talents. In addition to being a skillful artist and a clever writer, he had a way with the ladies and a knack for making friends where it could do him the most good.

The beautiful Madame de Pompadour, favorite of the king, admired him and requested that he be appointed curator of her valuable collection of gems and medals. His superior abilities and the favor he enjoyed at court led him into the diplomatic service. As the years went by he was stationed at various times in Russia, Sweden, Switzerland, and Italy.

His career was interrupted by the Revolution of 1789, which changed, if it did not end, the life of every aristocrat in France. Stripped of his lands and his income, Denon lived for years in poverty on the outskirts of Paris. In order to earn enough to eat, he resorted to his skill as an artist and was able occasionally to sell a drawing for a few sous.

Impoverished as he was, he had been an aristocrat and was fortunate in keeping his head while many of his aristocratic friends were losing theirs to the guillotine. In time his trained hand and his flair for getting on with people of influence led him to a job engraving the drawings of the famous artist Jacques Louis David, official painter of the Revolution who had studied in Rome and had been a disciple of Winckelmann and Newcastle.

Under David's patronage Denon once again sparkled

in Paris society, charmed the ladies with his smile and his wit, and made important new acquaintances—the most important of whom was the rising young General Bonaparte.

Since his childhood Denon had dreamed of someday making a voyage to Egypt. His busy life had kept him otherwise occupied, but when the chance came to accompany Napoleon's expeditionary force as an artist he gladly made the most of it.

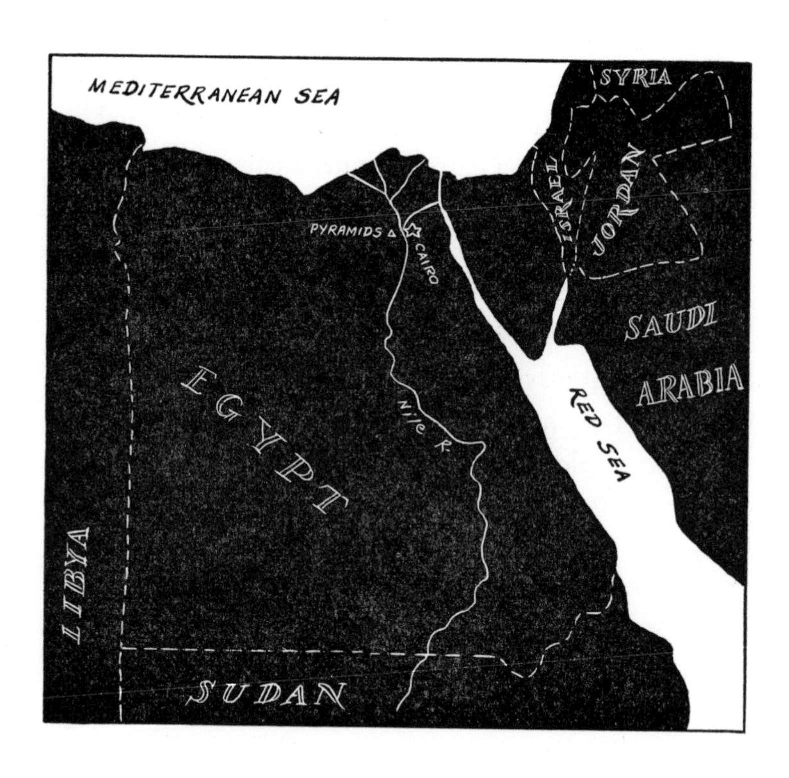

At the age of fifty-one he set out on the greatest adventure of his life. In Egypt he marched across the desert with the troops, bathed with them in the Nile, and camped with them before Cairo, close by the great stone pyramids of Giza.

The enemy's colorful army of dashing horsemen, commanded by Murad Bey, the turbaned ruler of Egypt, was no match for French fire power. The battle of Cairo turned into a bloody rout and Napoleon entered the city in triumph.

With the fighting all but over, the scientists and scholars were able to get at the business for which they had come. Denon was attached to the staff of General Desaix, whose assignment it was to lead an expedition in pursuit of the fleeing Murad Bey.

Riding with Desaix's force, Denon traveled the length of Egypt, from Cairo as far as the first cataract of the Nile, more than four hundred miles up the river. It was a journey into a lost world. Every day brought to view new landscapes in which stood the splendid ruins of temples and tombs so old that written history held no record of their origins.

In camp at night Denon made drawings of whatever ruins were nearby. He was so enraptured by all there was to be seen and recorded that he hardly noticed the hardships of the journey. When the enemy was en-

countered and a skirmish took place, the exuberant artist urged on the soldiers with a flourish of his rolled drawing paper. Then, realizing that the scene was subject matter for a picture, he began to sketch it, paying no more attention to the bullets than he would have had they been flies.

The walls of many structures were inscribed with intricate characters which apparently comprised the writing of the ancient Egyptian people. What long-kept secrets would be disclosed if only it were possible to read them! Denon copied the characters exactly as they were, even though he knew that nobody alive had any more idea than he did as to their meaning.

By the time he got back to Cairo his portfolio was bulging with drawings of the wonders he had seen. His colleagues, meanwhile, had been making measurements, records, plaster casts, and paintings of relics they had found in other parts of the country.

One of the most important of their discoveries was a piece of polished black stone on which was written an inscription in three languages—ancient Greek, ancient Egyptian, and later Egyptian. The stone was called the Rosetta stone, after the place near which it was found. Scholars were able to translate the Greek words. Hope ran high that in time it would be possible to figure out from their translation the meaning of the corresponding Egyptian words and so learn how to read the language that held the key to the history of the kings and the people who long ago occupied the land.

The task of studying and classifying all they had collected, to say nothing of figuring out what it meant and might contribute to the historic record, appeared so tremendous to Denon and his fellow workers that they knew it could not be completed in their lifetimes. And time, for the French in Egypt, was suddenly running out.

In spite of the army's initial victories, Napoleon's campaign failed. While he was taking possession of Cairo a British fleet, under Lord Nelson, had attacked and destroyed his ships. In the end the invaders had to give up everything they had won, their huge collection of antiquities as well as their conquered territory. Fortunately for the scholars they still had records, copies, and plaster casts and were able to send back to Paris enough material to keep them occupied at home for a long time to come.

If Napoleon's soldiers had not accomplished anything of lasting value in Egypt, his team of scientists had. Their investigations threw the light of scholarship on a civilization then believed to be the oldest in the world. The material they collected, including Dominique Vivant Denon's drawings, formed the basis for a twenty-four volume publication entitled *Description of Egypt.* Denon himself wrote a popular book called *Travels in Upper and Lower Egypt.* These works presented to awed readers a world that they hardly knew had once existed.

Enthusiasm for the marvelous culture of ancient Egypt, for its monumental architecture, its painting and sculpture, took the form of an international craze. But for all the temples, pyramids, and palaces standing on the banks of the Nile, Egypt was silent and the story of her ancient past a tantalizing secret as long as Egyptian writing was undecipherable.

3. The "Egyptian"

One of Napoleon's "donkeys" was a famous mathematician named Jean Baptiste Joseph Fourier. Upon returning to France after the campaign in Egypt, Fourier became the chief administrative officer of the newly formed department of Isère.

The capital of the new department was the ancient city of Grenoble, renowned as a center of learning. Being himself a learned man, Monsieur Fourier took a great deal of interest in the schools that were under his jurisdiction. One day, while he was inspecting the lycée, or high school, in Grenoble a pupil named Jean François Champollion was pointed out to him as the most brilliant boy in the school.

Champollion was eleven years old. His favorite subject was languages. He had already mastered Latin and Greek and was learning Hebrew. He was also deeply interested in everything that had to do with Egypt.

After a brief conversation with the boy, Monsieur Fourier was so impressed that he invited him to his house to see his Egyptian collection.

The visit turned out to be as memorable to the prefect as it was to the student. After examining every item, Jean François returned to the fragments of papyrus and stone tablets on which appeared the hieroglyphs that are the symbols of Egyptian writing. "Can anyone read them?" he asked.

Monsieur Fourier informed him that nobody could.

"I'm going to do it," said Jean François. "In a few years I will be able to. When I am big."

If it seemed like a large promise to come from such a small boy, it was not to be long before he was proving how earnestly he meant it. To prepare himself he studied every language that he thought might help solve the ultimate problem. When he was twelve he was reading the Old Testament in the original Hebrew. At thirteen he began to learn Arabic, Syrian, and Coptic, the last being the form of Egyptian which was spoken in early Christian times. He even studied Old Chinese to see if he could find any link to ancient Egyptian.

As he grew up he demonstrated a quality even more important to the realization of his ambition than the ability to learn difficult languages. He proved that he was also able to think for himself. While he was still a schoolboy he compiled an ingenious historical chart of ancient Egypt, based on references in the Bible and various old Latin, Arabic, and Hebrew texts. He furthermore proposed the outline for a book, to be called *Egypt Under the Pharaohs,* and wrote an introduction to it.

After graduating from the lycée in Grenoble, Champollion studied for two years in Paris. With his dark complexion and somewhat oriental features, to say nothing of his passion for all things pertaining to Egypt, he became known as "The Egyptian."

In Paris Champollion was able to turn his attention to the Rosetta stone. The original was in London, but he had access to pictures and facsimiles of it. He had already spent five or six years preparing himself for this undertaking, and yet he went about it slowly.

First he compared the characters on the stone with those on various papyri and tried to figure out what letters they represented. By doing this he had already come closer to success than most others who had puzzled over the meaning of Egyptian hieroglyphs. They had assumed that the characters comprised some kind of picture writing, whereas he looked at them as the symbols for spoken sounds, just as the letters of the alphabet are.

But further progress was slow and there was other work that demanded his attention. He returned to Grenoble, where he became a twenty-year-old professor of history. When he was not teaching he wrote plays, essays, and political songs and made plans for books. He compiled a Coptic dictionary and, in addition to everything else, took a great deal of interest in the turbulent politics of the time. Regardless of what political party was in power, however, he always held truth and freedom in high regard. During the last days of Napoleon's rule, his devotion to his high ideals got him into trouble with the authorities and he lost his job with the university.

With the termination of his teaching he at last had time to concentrate all his efforts on deciphering the Rosetta stone. The Greek translation of the inscription on the stone told that it was a decree proclaiming special divine honors to be granted King Ptolemy Epiphanes by the priesthood. In the text there appeared an oval ring, or cartouche, enclosing certain groups of characters. Champollion guessed that the purpose of the cartouche might be to emphasize an important word—and what word could be more important than the name of the king? In this way he learned what he assumed to be the characters for the name Ptolemy. By comparing these characters with the oval enclosed names of rulers appearing in other texts, he proved himself right. Having learned a few symbols and established a system, he was able to enlarge his knowledge of the hieroglyphs and the letters they represented until he at last was master of the language.

Such an explanation, of course, is an oversimplification of a problem so difficult that it took a linguistic genius years of thought and study to solve it. When he at last succeeded, the words of the Egyptians themselves could tell the story of the splendid civilization that once had flourished along the Nile.

In 1828, having made his great contribution to Egyptian archaeology without leaving France, Champollion led an expedition to Egypt. There he and his colleagues spent a year and a half studying, copying, and translating inscriptions that had been written three and four thousand years before. The modern Egyptians looked with awe on the man who could read the hieroglyphs and welcomed him warmly to their country.

Jean François Champollion died three years after returning from Egypt. After his death overcautious critics challenged the validity of his discovery. Time, however, was to prove that he had correctly deciphered the Egyptian hieroglyphs. A century later his great achievement is considered by many authorities to be the starting point in the development of the modern science of archaeology.

4. Pioneers of a New Science

IN THE EARLY 1800s archaeology was still a game for explorers and collectors, a form of treasure hunting more than a profession for scientists.

Napoleon's and Champollion's expeditions aroused so much interest in ancient Egypt that many museums became buyers of Egyptian antiquities. The second wave of explorers to invade the land of the Nile was made up largely of collectors who came principally to study the relics so that they might learn what was transportable for sale to the waiting museums abroad.

Antique hunting on such a grand scale was an adventurous pastime. It appealed to inquiring minds and strong constitutions. At the same time the image, resurrected from Egypt's ruins, of a once-splendid and long-lost civilization increased the appetites of both scholars and the public for further knowledge of man's early history.

Did not the Bible tell of nations as old as Egypt? The valley of Mesopotamia, between the Euphrates and the Tigris rivers in what is today Iraq, was known by tradition to be the land of the once-powerful Assyrians and the even earlier Babylonians.

Not many Europeans visited Mesopotamia in the nineteenth century. Those who did were impressed by the numerous strange mounds that stood up from the dusty desert plains. One of the most astute early investigators of the region was a young Englishman named Claudius James Rich. Between 1811 and 1820 he made a number of excursions from Baghdad, where he was stationed as a member of the council for the East India Company, to the mounds of Mesopotamia. He subsequently wrote and published several books about them. But not until the 1840s were the mounds opened to determine what they concealed.

The first to excavate was Paul Émile Botta, French

consul at Mosul. Digging at Khorsabad, once called Dur Sharrukin, near the Tigris River, he uncovered the terraced palaces of Assyrian kings, their walls decorated with reliefs of hunters and warriors and their portals guarded by stone statues of winged lions. Scattered in the rubble were hundreds of clay tablets and cylinders on which were inscribed, in characters that looked like closely spaced bird tracks, an undecipherable literature. A brilliant explorer named Major Henry Creswicke Rawlinson studied the script called cuneiform and eventually was able to read the names of kings and places and accounts of events, some of which duplicated parts of the text of the Old Testament.

Soon other excavations were being undertaken in the same vicinity. An adventurous traveler, Austen Henry Layard, uncovered the ruins of Nineveh, once the Assyrian capital. The discoveries of Botta, Layard, and Rawlinson helped show that the Old Testament account of the Assyrians had an archaeological basis. They also stimulated archaeological thinking and activity in other countries.

Remains and relics of prehistoric man were found to be lying under heel in the well-trod earth of the British Isles and northern and central Europe. At the same time that excavators were digging in the Old World, an American lawyer and amateur antiquarian

named John Lloyd Stephens proved that civilization in the New World was not as new as had been previously assumed. Deep in the jungles of Central America he found huge stone pyramids and temples of the highly developed culture of the Mayan Indians which flourished long before the first white men settled in America.

Not all the pioneers of archaeology, however, were explorers with shovels. A Danish businessman whose principal interest in life was the establishment and growth of a national museum in Copenhagen made a contribution to the new science that was as important as any discovery in the field.

His name was Christian Thomsen. He was born in 1788 in Copenhagen, where his father was a well-to-do merchant and shipowner. While still a boy Christian went to work in the family business. He also collected old coins and established a local reputation as a dedicated antiquarian. When he was twenty-seven years old, the newly formed Commission for the Preservation of Danish Antiquities elected him secretary. His principal duty was to classify and arrange for display the hundreds of historic and prehistoric objects in the commission's collection.

Having had no previous experience in handling such a rare and ancient inventory, he devised his own procedure, based on methods learned in his father's warehouses. He divided the collection into objects made of stone, of metal, and of pottery, and then subdivided them into tools, weapons, and utensils. As he grew more and more familiar with the objects and their classification, it occurred to him that those made of stone were almost invariably older than those made of metal.

Until this time all relics that were believed to belong to a period before the beginning of recorded history had been vaguely classified as prehistoric, often without any clear idea of their order of origin. As Thomsen worked in the museum, devoting to it all his spare time and eventually retiring from business to become its director, he established a system which consigned all prehistoric relics to one of three ages—the primitive *Stone Age,* in which only stone was used for tools and weapons because the use of metal was unknown; the later *Bronze Age,* when copper and bronze were the only metals in general use; or the *Iron Age,* which extends into modern times. Thus a sequence was established, based on the various degrees of technical proficiency attained by ancient cultures.

As a result of the Three Age System, archaeologists, digging in the ground and finding human bones and stone axes together in one place, could reasonably assume that the site was older than one containing human bones and bronze swords. For the first time they had a method to help them determine *how* old in relationship to each other were the old things they were finding.

Improved techniques and methods were helping to make a systematic science of this search for the remains of bygone civilizations. But for all its advances toward scientific method, archaeology was still a field of knowledge and exploration full of surprise and adventure, as demonstrated by the wonderful adventures of Heinrich Schliemann in his quest for the lost city of ancient Troy.

5. With Homer for His Guide

ON A BITTER NIGHT in 1841 a December gale sank a German trading brig in the North Sea off the coast of Holland. The next morning one of the survivors, naked, bleeding, and half frozen, was washed up on shore.

Upon being questioned he identified himself as Heinrich Schliemann, nineteen years old, lately of Hamburg, Germany, from which city he had been bound for Venezuela when the ship in which he was a passenger ran into foul weather and foundered.

He was taken to a hospital and treated for cuts and exposure. When he was discharged, the German consul in Amsterdam assured him that arrangements would be made for sending him back to Hamburg.

But Heinrich Schliemann did not want to go back. The boyhood he was leaving behind had little hold on him. Only by recalling its earliest years could he find any joy in his memories. It seemed a long and difficult lifetime ago since he had leaned on his father's knee, listening wide-eyed to wonderful stories of ancient history.

His father had told him about Pompeii, and explained that the buried city was being slowly uncovered. And he had told him exciting tales about the gods and heroes of ancient Greece. Heinrich's favorite was the story of how the Greeks, led by Agamemnon, king of Mycenae, captured Troy. He even had a picture book that showed the citadel in flames. When he asked if Troy really looked the way the picture showed it, his father had told him that nobody really knew. Troy was long gone and with it all traces of where it had once stood.

Then and there the seven-year-old boy had made up his mind that someday he was going to find the lost city of Troy.

The harsh realities of existence, however, had made him all but forget the childhood dream. His mother had died. At the age of fourteen he had to quit school and go to work as apprentice to a grocer. After five years of drudgery he had made his way to the big city of Hamburg to seek his fortune. There he learned of a position that was open in South America. He accepted it, embarked for the New World, and two weeks later was shipwrecked en route.

Once in Holland he decided to stay. He found a job with an Amsterdam merchant. By working hard and living frugally he not only got ahead in business but also was able to apply himself to furthering his education.

He had a special talent for languages. Studying in his spare time, he could learn to speak and write a new language in six weeks. One after another he mastered Dutch, English, French, Spanish, Italian, Portuguese, and eventually Russian.

At the same time he studied everything that had a bearing on merchandising. He became such a good businessman that his firm sent him to Russia as its agent. There he went into business for himself. Before he was forty years old he had amassed a fortune.

Ambitious though he was to make money, he felt a need for the richness that can be gained only by increasing the resources of the mind. He continued to read and study, learning new languages until he knew eighteen. In his business journeys to many countries he visited libraries and museums and conferred with scholars. In London he discovered the British Museum and was fascinated by the large collection of relics from ancient Egypt. At home, in his own library, he spent Sundays reading Homer in the original Greek. He loved scholarship and was especially moved by all that pertained to the golden age of Greece. He read again, this time in the Greek poet's own words, about the siege of Troy, and he brooded over his childhood boast that someday he would find the place where it had stood.

At last he resolved to retire from business. In 1864, at the age of forty-two, he gave up his career as a merchant to devote himself to study and exploration.

He began his new life by going around the world. When the trip was over he settled in Paris to study archaeology. He profited by the lessons to be learned from the professional archaeologists, but in addition to absorbing their ideas he continued to study his beloved Homer and to accept the poet's description of ancient Troy as accurate historic and geographic fact.

Such faith in the words of a bard who was himself all but legendary was scoffed at by practical-minded and unimaginative scholars. Yet with Homer as his guide, the retired merchant went to Asia Minor and

found what he was looking for—and more. Helped by the young Greek bride whom he married when he was in his forties, and by crews of Greek and Turkish workmen, he dug at the site which he believed answered to Homer's description.

Under the ground he found layer upon layer of ancient ruins which dated back beyond Roman times and yet did not belong to the great days of Greece. Impatiently he kept his workers digging, slicing through unidentified walls and foundations to get at even more deeply buried remains. The fulfillment of a lifetime of work, study, dreaming, and waiting was at stake.

After two arduous seasons of excavation, Schliemann was rewarded by the discovery of a layer of ashes and charred ruins which comprised the long-buried remains of a devastating fire. This, he concluded, was where King Priam's Troy had stood, and where it had finally fallen before the torch and the sword of the crafty invaders who entered the city hidden in the belly of a wooden horse.

Having uncovered the lost city of Troy and taken a treasure, both in historic data and in gleaming gold, from the ruins, Schliemann shifted his operations back across the Aegean Sea to Greece. He dug at Mycenae, once Agamemnon's home, and at nearby Tiryns, bringing to light remains of an Aegean culture that had flourished long before Homer's heroes walked the earth.

News of the finds thrilled the world. Heinrich Schliemann continued to search in the ground, applying to his excavations many of the methods that other archaeologists had found successful in Egypt and Mesopotamia. The scientific value of his work increased from year to year as he grew in experience and employed trained men to help him.

Outstanding among his assistants was a German architect and archaeologist named Wilhelm Dörpfeld. Before working with Schliemann, young Dörpfeld had

dug in Greece with a German expedition under Ernst Curtius. Dörpfeld's thoroughness often tried the patience of Schliemann, who, as Joan Evans, in *Time and Chance*, the biography of her father Arthur Evans, has said, ". . . seemed to wrest things from the earth by force of enthusiasm." But the younger man's methods, added to his employer's intuition, greatly increased the scientific value of the work they did together.

Hardly anything had been known about the prehistory of Greece until Schliemann uncovered Troy and Mycenae. His discoveries proved that the Homeric poems were not mere fiction, but were about people who had actually lived, places that really existed, and events that once took place.

In the last years of his life Schliemann contemplated new fields to conquer. He wondered if the unexplored ruins scattered over the nearby island of Crete might be the remains of an earlier civilization from which Mycenae and Tiryns had sprung. He visited Crete and negotiated to buy a piece of land on which extensive ruins were known to be buried. The landowner asked such an exorbitant price, however, that the transaction fell through.

Heinrich Schliemann died in 1890. After his death excavation and study at Troy was continued under the direction of Dörpfeld. As the rubble of nine layers

of buried towns was re-examined, it was found that Homer's Troy was not the second from the bottom, as Schliemann had thought, but the *sixth* from the bottom. The discoverer of Troy had dug right through the ruins of the city he was looking for and found the remains of five earlier towns, the first and deepest of which went back almost a thousand years before the times and events that Homer wrote about in the *Iliad*—back to a world so ancient that to archaeology and the modern world it was entirely new.

6. The Curious General

SCHLIEMANN'S ADVENTURES opened new approaches to antiquity and proved that the writers of ancient times wrote more truth than they had generally been given credit for. Some archaeologists and scholars, however, were critical of his methods and denounced them as being haphazard and unscientific.

The fact is that not many archaeologists were yet equipped with sound technique and those who wished for better sometimes had to teach themselves. One antiquarian who lived at the same time as Schliemann taught himself so well that he set an example for others and left archaeology a more exact science than he found it.

He was a British army officer named Augustus Henry Lane Fox. He had served with distinction in the Crimean War, but the principal achievement of his military career was his study and improvement of the army rifle in the 1850s. The study of small arms involved him in the history of weapons, which in turn led him into a special but nonetheless significant aspect of archaeology—the evolution not only of weapons but also of all the ordinary, everyday objects produced by various cultures.

In a London house already brimming with a large family which included six growing sons and three daughters, he assembled a collection of hundreds of objects—weapons, tools, boats, articles of clothing, musical instruments, and many other things—that eventually covered the walls and crowded all the rooms from cellar to attic.

The items were not chosen, as are most objects cherished by collectors, for beauty or rarity but, on the contrary, because they were ordinary and typical of *all* the things made and used by given peoples at various times. "Common things are of more importance than particular things, because they are more prevalent," the old soldier liked to say. The remark explained the true value of the collection. It was significant because it facilitated study of the complete material equipment of a culture and encouraged comparison of one culture to another.

This unique approach, recognized by many of Lane Fox's scholarly friends and acquaintances for what it was worth, formed the basis for a method of comparative analysis in archaeology. The general was honored by being made a Fellow of the Royal Society, vice-president of the Society of Antiquaries, and president of the Anthropological Institute. His collection was moved out of the crowded house in London and installed first at South Kensington and finally at Oxford, in the University Museum.

In 1880 Lane Fox inherited a fortune from his great-uncle, George Pitt. Under the terms of the will he became master of Rushmore, a huge country estate, and took the name Pitt-Rivers. Retiring from the army with the rank of lieutenant general at the age of fifty-five, he devoted the rest of his life to scientific research.

On his land there was a deer preserve known as Cranborne Chase, where prehistoric earthworks and grave mounds remained intact because the ground above and around them had never been broken by the plow. Here he undertook to excavate the remains of Roman-British villages and fortifications. In so doing he made his second valuable contribution to archaeology.

Being a military man, the General organized his digging projects along strict military lines and carried them out with the thoroughness of a good field officer. Because excavation, by its very nature, usually meant destruction of the site being studied, he trained his staff to record every detail of each day's work. Trenches were dug with a mathematical exactness few excavators had ever taken the trouble to carry out. The carefully excavated walls of the precise trenches laid bare, in cross section, layer upon layer of earth and rubble

belonging to successive past periods. These layers, called stratification by archaeologists, could then be studied and photographed, and their sequence, contents, and characteristics recorded in writing. Precise models were made of every excavation. After a site had been completely dug up, there remained drawings, plans, cross sections, and photographs to record permanently each phase of the operation and form the basis for prompt publication of the final results.

It is not surprising that in his day the wealthy old General was considered something of an eccentric. As if his eternal digging and his meticulous concern for detail were not unusual enough, he attempted to raise llamas and yaks and he established private schools expressly for the purpose of educating the wild, dark-eyed children of the numerous gypsies who squatted on his broad British estates.

The methods evolved and practiced by the General were unusual for his time. Other archaeologists might happen across ancient and valuable objects in the ground, but as far as he was concerned the unearthing of history was not a casual treasure hunt, presided over by chance. On the contrary it was strictly a matter of scientific research. To this day modern archaeological excavation employs many of the methods established by General Pitt-Rivers.

7. Excavator of Knossos

CRETE IS A LONG, NARROW ISLAND in the Mediterranean Sea. Homer described it in the *Odyssey* with the following words:

"Out in the dark blue sea there lies a land called Crete, a rich and lovely land, washed by the waves on every side, densely peopled and boasting ninety cities . . . . One of the ninety towns is a great city called Knossos."

Heinrich Schliemann had visited the island in search

of the origins of the culture he found at Mycenae. He looked toward Crete because its terrain was littered with unexplored ruins and because its position, almost equidistant between Asia Minor, Greece, and Egypt, suggested that it might have been a steppingstone connecting these three centers of early civilization.

Had Schliemann lived long enough, perhaps he would have added "the great city called Knossos" to his conquests. As it was, the honor went to an English archaeologist named Arthur Evans.

In 1894 Evans paid his first visit to Crete. At the age of forty-three he was well known to intellectuals in England as the son of a distinguished amateur scien-

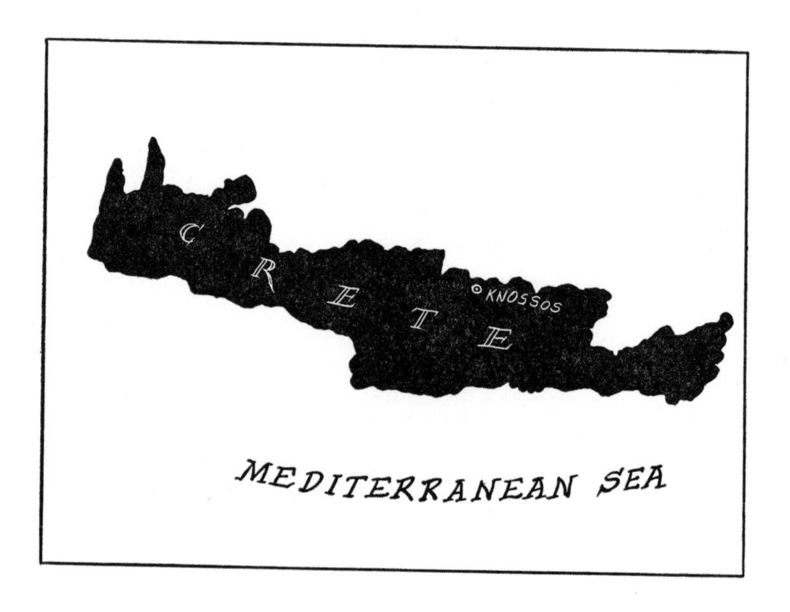

tist and, in his own right, as a scholar, traveler, newspaper correspondent, archaeologist, and keeper of the Ashmolean Museum of Art and Archaeology at Oxford.

He was a restless, questing, determined sort of man, small of stature, trim and strong, who liked to travel on foot through wild country and never minded spending a night wherever darkness happened to find him. He had lived for a number of adventurous years in the Balkans and had been a bold spokesman for the cause of freedom in those southern Slavic countries which were struggling against Austrian oppression. Half of his full, rich life was behind him. His beloved wife, who had been his companion in many of his travels and a helper in his work, was dead. But the years that still lay ahead were to be the most productive and significant of his long career.

During his travels he had been to Greece. There he visited Schliemann and was shown the treasures found at Troy and Mycenae. And of all the wonderful things he looked at, those that most interested him were a few cut stones the size of beads.

Evans was nearsighted. In order to see anything small he had to hold it close to his eyes. Then he could see it so clearly that it was almost as though he were looking through a magnifying glass. Examining the tiny gems with his microscope-like eyes, he was surprised to find that they were covered with engraved marks that resembled hieroglyphs. He began to wonder if the early Aegean people whose towns and fortresses Schliemann was uncovering might have possessed a written language.

A few years later, on another visit to Athens, he found similarly engraved stones for sale in certain antique shops. The dealers told him that they came from Crete. So to Crete he went, in search of further examples of the mysterious script.

Everywhere he went, even in the most remote parts of the island, there were remains of a once flourishing civilization. In some respects the ruins looked like those of Mycenae, but apparently they were even older. As for the engraved stones—they were so plentiful that peasant women wore them around their necks as charms.

By the time Evans left Crete he was so struck with wonder and curiosity that he was not able to stay away for long. He returned several times during the next few years. Eventually he obtained official permission to dig at a site where preliminary superficial investigations on the part of several archaeological enthusiasts had indicated the probable existence of extensive buried ruins. It was generally believed that this might be the site of Knossos, prehistoric capital of Crete.

Under Arthur Evans' direction, and largely at his own expense, excavation was begun in 1899. In nine weeks two acres of ruins were uncovered, revealing the rooms, courtyards, stairs, and passageways of an elaborate palace. Among the rubble of crumbling walls were found not only hundreds of clay tablets inscribed with undecipherable hieroglyphs similar to those on the stone seals Schliemann had taken from the ruins of Mycenae but also many fragments of beautifully painted frescoes and stuccoed reliefs. One mural painting depicted an acrobat somersaulting over the horns of a charging bull. The same scene was engraved on seals and fashioned in the form of ivory statuettes.

Painting, sculpture, and architecture told a vivid story of what the early Cretans had looked like, how they had dressed, and what their daily activities were.

From the extensive ruins and rich remains that came to light as the excavating went on year after year, Evans was able to piece together a picture of the elaborate society that had existed on Crete long before Mycenae had flourished. He estimated that the beginnings of Crete as a civilized state went back more than four thousand years to a time when Egypt was still young. From the evidence of Egyptian artifacts found among the ruins of Knossos it was apparent that Crete had traded with Egypt and through this trade Egyptian influences had entered Aegean culture.

Evans called the civilization of Crete *Minoan,* after King Minos, who, according to Greek legend, was the kingdom's greatest monarch. Archaeological evidence showed that it had been an affluent nation, a great sea power, and a center of commerce for nearly two thousand years. In the end the palaces and towns were destroyed by some catastrophe so violent that the people were unable to rally and build them up again. Some scholars believed that a terrible earthquake, followed by fire, had put an end to Minoan glory. Others thought that an invasion from the northern mainland might have brought about Crete's final fall.

Perhaps further research will someday clarify these tumultuous and long-forgotten events. Until such a time they must remain among history's many unsolved mysteries.

By undertaking the leadership in archaeological exploration of Crete, Arthur Evans extended the record of Aegean civilization back a thousand years beyond the frontier established by Schliemann's discoveries of Troy and Mycenae. Under his direction parts of the palace at Minos were rebuilt. The only lasting disappointment of his decades of research at Knossos was that he never succeeded in deciphering the Minoan script. His example and his accomplishments, however, profoundly affected succeeding generations of scholars and helped them continue the search for answers to problems which he himself never solved. As the Grand Old Man of archaeology he was knighted for his contributions to science and lived to enjoy his position as one of the foremost men in his field until he was ninety. His prestige in his own country was so great that from the time he began excavating at Knossos until the present, archaeology has been a particularly popular subject in England and a large proportion of the world's leading modern archaeologists have been, and are, Englishmen.

8. "Inch by Inch"

WILLIAM MATTHEW FLINDERS PETRIE was a handsome and bearded young archaeologist of twenty-seven when he arrived in Egypt from England for the first time in 1880. He had come for the purpose of making exact measurements of the tombs of the Pharaohs.

The first thing he did after inspecting the pyramids of Giza, just outside Cairo, was to select a convenient tomb and set up housekeeping in it so that he could be near his work. Every evening, when the last of the tourists left the great pyramid, he would enter it. Removing all his clothes for greater comfort, he would often spend half the night measuring airless chambers and passageways—their length and breadth and cross section, the angles of their corners, and the gradient of their floors.

Petrie was guided in all he did by the same kind of conscientiousness and self-imposed high standards that made Pitt-Rivers a pioneer of truly scientific archaeology. His enthusiasm for measuring and for ancient ruins dated back to his childhood. Poor health had kept him from going to school. His early education took place at home in London where he absorbed from a brilliant mother and father, and from his own reading, a wide range of interests and learning. A favorite great-aunt also played an important role in his upbringing and instilled in him a strong respect for the past. Years later he was to write of her in his autobiography, *Seventy Years of Archaeology:* "She talked of the college days of her father, about 1770, and was full of the stirring events of her youth, of the adored Nelson, and the watch, night by night, for the beacons on the Lincolnshire Coast which might signal Napoleon's invasion."

An aptitude for mathematics prompted the boy to teach himself geometry and trigonometry. He was especially interested in the practical application of mathematics to problems of physical measurement. At the same time he took an early interest in antiquity. On being told by another boy of the unearthing of a Roman villa on the Isle of Wight in the English Channel, he was horrified to hear of the rough way it was dug up. Even at the age of eight he knew, as he later wrote, that "the earth ought to be poured away inch by inch, to see all that was in it and how it lay."

As a young man Petrie began his archaeological researches by surveying and measuring the prehistoric Saxon and Roman relics of southern Britain. One of these was the mysterious circle of massive stones known as Stonehenge. He wrote a book about Stonehenge which was published the year he went abroad to begin his field work in Egypt.

The idea for the journey to Egypt originated with his father, who was obsessed with the supposed mystic significances of the pyramids and proposed that they go together to measure and study them. But as time passed, the elder William Petrie's affairs continued to delay him at home until at last young William realized that if ever he were going he would have to go alone.

In the half-century between Champollion's departure from Egypt and Petrie's arrival, world-wide interest in the valley of the Nile and its ancient civilization had brought many enthusiasts flocking to the scene.

First there had been the collectors, such as Giovanni Belzoni, an Italian adventurer and jack-of-many-trades who arrived in Egypt even before Champollion and whose chief motive was to send every movable object of value back to the museums of Europe. This kind of "collecting," which was no better than plundering, shocked all honest scholars. The foremost Egyptologist in the mid-1840s was the German scholar Karl Richard Lepsius. He was the first archaeologist to look beneath the surfaces, to dig and measure, to catalogue and make order out of the chaos of ruins and relics with which the Egyptian earth was heaped. He was followed by Auguste Mariette, who arrived in Egypt from Paris in 1850 and devoted thirty years to finding, studying, and preserving the antiquities of the country.

When Petrie began to work in Egypt, Mariette was seventy-four years old and still digging. The reputation and achievements of the older man notwithstanding, Petrie was as scornful of Mariette's methods as he was of those of most of his predecessors. In his opinion the archaeologists and collectors of the past had dug up the great things but had not taken enough trouble to study the small things. They had too often failed to apply systematic scientific method to their research, with the result that they had irrevocably destroyed many valuable clues to Egypt's lost history. He set out to remedy the situation in his own way. When he dug he took care not to injure what he was uncovering. He always kept future investigators of the site in mind. He meticulously measured every architectural remain and ancient object he found. And he published full descriptions and records of all monuments and excavations as soon as possible after completing his studies of them.

He was a man of action and steadfast determination. When he decided to open an unidentified pyramid located at a remote spot near the Nile, and was unable to find an entrance in the customary place, he had his workmen chop a narrow passageway straight through the masonry. After weeks of work the burial vault was reached. A boy carrying a light was lowered into the vault on a rope. There he found two empty sarcophagi. The tomb had long ago been entered and robbed.

A less resolute archaeologist might have credited the time lost to experience and let it go at that. But not Petrie. The passageway was made large enough for him to enter. Water had seeped into the vault. He scraped through muck and dirt until he found an alabaster vat bearing the name of Amenemhet III, a great king of the Twelfth Dynasty who had reigned from 1849 to 1801 B.C. Even after having identified the tomb, Petrie continued to study it. He crawled through sti-

fling passageways, dead-end tunnels, and dark, doorless chambers in an effort to determine how the ancient robbers had found their way into the tomb. It was a riddle he never could explain. But he did find the entrance, located, as it turned out, on the south instead of the usual north side of the pyramid. It was characteristic of his thoroughness and diligence that he devoted himself to the undertaking until he had learned from it every bit of knowledge that could possibly be obtained.

As the years went by, his excavations were not confined to Egypt. In 1890 he undertook a short season of exploration in Palestine, where he was eventually to spend much time and do much of his work. With the passing of season after season his methods, his accomplishments in the field, and his many publications brought him increasingly wide recognition.

The great Schliemann paid him a visit when he was excavating the pyramid of Hawara in Egypt. In *Seventy Years of Archaeology* Petrie wrote the following word picture of the aging German scholar: "Schliemann, short, round-headed, round-faced, round-hatted, great round-goggle-eyed, spectacled, cheeriest of beings; dogmatic, but always ready for facts."

Summers, when the fiery desert heat made it impossible to work in the field, he usually spent in England. There he arranged for exhibiting recent finds and prepared his reports for publication. In 1892 he was appointed professor of Egyptology at University College, London. Five years later, at the age of forty-four, he married the charming artist Hilda Urlin, whom he met at the college. The following winter they spent their honeymoon digging together in Egypt.

By 1900 Petrie, although still a relatively young man, had done more excavating in Egypt than any other archaeologist has done in a lifetime. He examined the soil "inch by inch" to sift out the remains of three thousand pre-Christian years of human habitation. The search uncovered graves and artifacts that went back to a distant time before the first of the great Pharaohs, when Egypt was not yet a strong, united kingdom. It brought to light the first Mycenaean objects found in Egypt, thereby corroborating the evidence that trade existed between the Nile and the Aegean as originally suggested by Arthur Evans' finds of Egyptian objects in Crete. From the pottery, artifacts, tools, and many objects he acquired during a lifetime of field work, Petrie evolved a time sequence that made it possible for him to establish a chronological order to ancient Egyptian history.

He was knighted in 1923 in recognition of his outstanding archaeological achievements. In his old age he traveled and roughed it as vigorously as he had in his youth. He lived to be eighty-nine. While he lay on his deathbed in Palestine, during World War II, he was visited by a friend, Mortimer Wheeler, then a British army officer but in civilian life one of the foremost of England's younger archaeologists. In his autobiography, *Still Digging*, Wheeler was to write of his last visit with the noble old gentleman, "The picture of him is stamped in my mind. He was swathed in white sheets, and a sort of turban of white linen was about his head. His grey beard and superb profile gave him the aspect of a biblical patriarch."

9. Orientalist from the West

WHILE FLINDERS PETRIE was excavating near Thebes in the winter of 1894 he was visited by a pair of young American newlyweds, Dr. and Mrs. James Henry Breasted.

The Breasteds were enjoying a honeymoon cruise on the Nile aboard a chartered river boat. The voyage was a combination of pleasure and work. James Breasted, from Illinois, was an Egyptologist who had just received his degree after three years of study at the University of Berlin. His bride was a California girl who had also been recently studying in Berlin. Their honeymoon in Egypt was a farewell to the Old World before returning to the United States where a job as instructor of Egyptology awaited Dr. Breasted at the newly established University of Chicago.

Meeting Flinders Petrie and spending a week with him was a highlight of the journey. For his part the distinguished veteran of fourteen seasons in Egypt was so impressed by the young scholar that he invited him to share the leadership of a subsequent expedition.

Breasted was flattered at the offer, but excavation was not his specialty. The task he had set for himself, in addition to the bread-and-butter business of teaching, was to read and accurately translate all known Egyptian inscriptions and reconstruct from them a complete history of Egypt.

In a letter to his mother and father in Chicago he wrote: "I want to read to my fellow men the *oldest* chapter in the story of human progress. I would rather do this than gain countless wealth."

Upon his return to Chicago in the spring of 1895 Dr. Breasted became the first instructor of Egyptology in an American university. His salary was only $800 a year and in order to support himself and his family he had to earn additional money by giving lectures. This meant a full schedule of hard work, but it did not keep him from what he was to write of in later years as ". . . one of the most arduous undertakings of my life . . . . I began the task of collecting all the historical sources of ancient Egypt, from the earliest times to the Persian conquest, wherever they existed in the world; of translating them into English; and of creating thereby for the first time a solid foundation of documentary source material for the production of a modern history of ancient Egypt."

The search, which had begun with a honeymoon cruise up the Nile, was to last for many years. On repeated leaves of absence from the university Dr.

Breasted, traveling with his wife and son, tracked down Egyptian inscriptions in museums, libraries, and private collections all over Europe, throughout the lands around the Mediterranean, and among the ruins of Egypt.

He became a kind of scholar-gypsy. It was a difficult life, for there was little money or comfort involved and a great deal of hard work. Back in the United States, where Egyptology still seemed to most people an obscure subject, support and appreciation were slow to materialize. But as the years passed, his travels, his researches, and the publications resulting from them created a steadily growing public interest.

From inscriptions and writings produced by the ancient Egyptians themselves, Breasted collected the material for his monumental *History of Egypt* published in 1905. This book was the first authentic Egyptian history by an American author. It not only brought to students and the public the facts of the ancient world as the archaeologist knew them, but it also made ancient times real, human, and nonmythological. The Egyptians who built the pyramids were presented as flesh-and-blood people with problems and emotions similar to those which people have today. Breasted's *History of Egypt* has gone through many printings in the last half-century and is still being used today.

In 1906 and 1907 his Egyptian source texts were published in five volumes under the title *Ancient Records of Egypt.* He soon began to be in demand as a lecturer all over the country. Americans, until recently too busy establishing their own civilization in an unsettled country to care about anything so remote as ancient Egypt, were beginning to find time to be curious about other places and former times.

Always, however, the young professor was up against the problem of money, both for his daily existence and for the support of his work. When a publishing company asked him to write a school text on ancient history he could not afford to ignore the offer. The resulting book, entitled *Ancient Times,* was published in 1916. It was to bring him an adequate income for the first time in his life and be instrumental in helping him secure financial backing for his future archaeological projects.

Ancient Times earned its author not only money but wider renown and greater prestige. He became known as the foremost Egyptologist in the United States. He was able to prevail upon John D. Rockefeller, Jr., to donate funds to establish a laboratory for the study of ancient civilizations. Founded in 1919 and called the Oriental Institute of the University of Chicago, it was the first organization of its kind.

As director of the Oriental Institute Dr. Breasted was at last able to go to Egypt and the Middle East with adequate money to purchase valuable antiquities and the authority to plan for future expeditions. Furthermore, it was his good fortune to take part in a dig that resulted in the most amazing archaeological discovery since Schliemann found Troy.

As one of a small and privileged group Breasted was present at the opening of the tomb of King Tutankhamen. The tomb had remained undiscovered long after the burying place of virtually every important monarch in ancient Egyptian history was accounted for. It was found by the British archaeologist Howard Carter. For many years he persisted in digging and searching in the Valley of the Kings, near the town of Luxor, where it seemed that every inch of ground had already been probed and combed through, until he finally came upon the sealed entrance to a tomb that had eluded the shovels of all previous excavators.

In the autumn of 1922, while Dr. Breasted was traveling in Egypt with his family, he received a message from Lord Carnarvon, the wealthy sponsor of Howard Carter, announcing an important find in the Valley of the Kings. Breasted went immediately to the site, which soon was to become the center of world-wide attention.

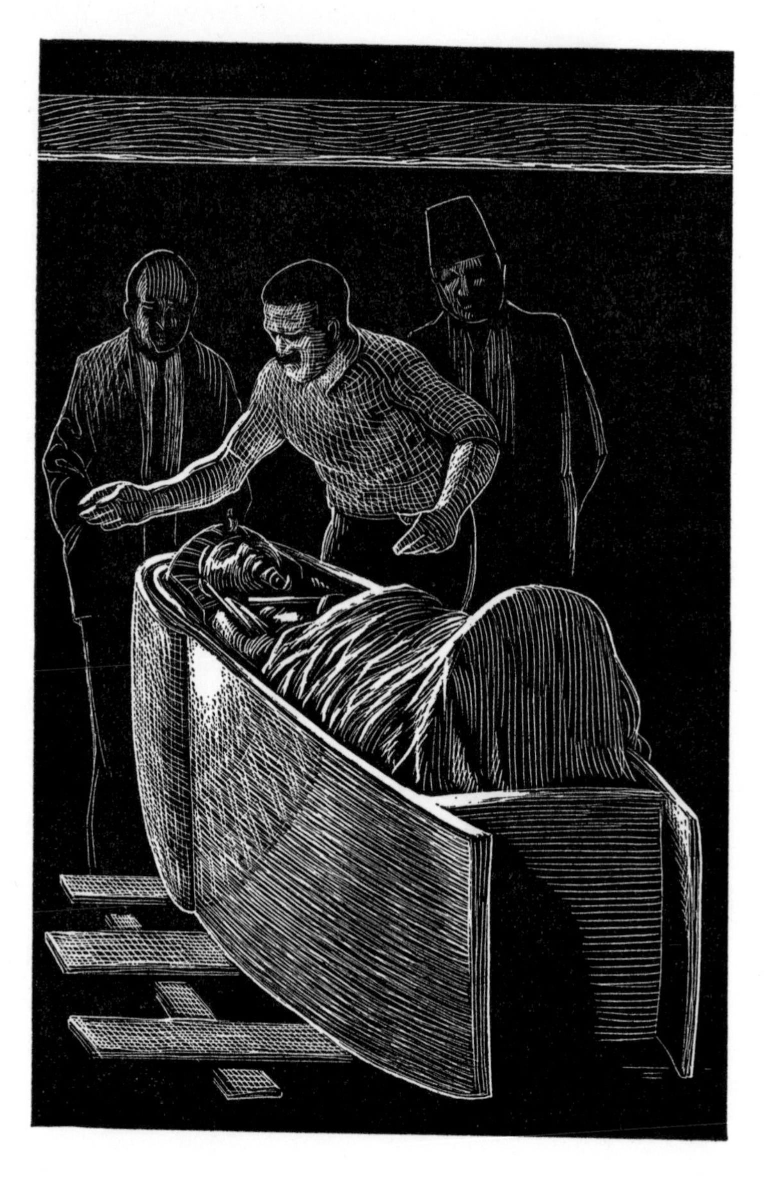

Like practically every other Egyptian tomb, that of King Tutankhamen had been broken into by grave robbers in ancient times. But the robbers had apparently been interrupted in their work and had fled with only a small amount of loot. The remaining contents comprised a dazzling inventory such as had never before been found in Egypt. Royal furniture, caskets of jewelry, vases made of alabaster, ornate chariots and huge pieces of statuary filled the several chambers of the tomb in a magnificent jumble. In the burial chamber, enclosed in a series of coffins, the last of which was made of solid gold, reposed the body of a boy king which had lain there 3250 years.

The contents of King Tutankhamen's tomb comprised one of the most beautiful and valuable ancient treasures ever unearthed. But to James Henry Breasted, who had devoted his career to bringing a clearer understanding of Egypt's ancient civilization to a twentieth-century public, the greatest value of the discovery lay in the world-wide interest in archaeology, and particularly in Egyptology, which it aroused. It was due to his scholarship, his writings, and his teaching no less than to such sensational discoveries as King Tutankhamen's tomb that the land of the Nile and its remains of former splendor no longer seemed as remote and unreal to modern Americans as they did when he was a struggling young scholar. Today the Oriental Institute is the greatest laboratory of its kind in the world. The researches that come from it perpetuate its founder's efforts to enlarge the knowledge and understanding of man's past achievements.

As an archaeologist Breasted was first and foremost an interpreter of archaeological evidence, a historian with the gift of being able to make the past live by relating it to the present. His writings and teachings led to a clearer understanding of man in his world and inspired younger archaeologists to the further study of history in terms of the lasting significant human values.

10. Old Ruins in the New World

THE ANCIENT PAST which James Henry Breasted helped make real to the twentieth century belonged to Egypt and to one of the earliest societies to achieve the state of order and technological proficiency known as civilization. It belonged to the Old World. But the New World also has an ancient past.

The story of American archaeology begins more than a hundred years ago. One of its earliest explorers was a lawyer, writer, traveler, and archaeologist from the state of New Jersey, John Lloyd Stephens.

In 1822, when he was only seventeen years old, Stephens was graduated from Columbia College. He studied law and for nearly a decade practiced as a lawyer in New York City. In 1834 he went abroad and for two years traveled in Europe, Russia, and the Middle East. The outstanding result of this odyssey was a book, published soon after his return to New York. It was called *Incidents of Travel in Arabia Petraea.*

The book was so well received by the critics and so widely read by the public that its author was encouraged to follow it up with two more travel volumes: *Incidents of Travel in Greece, Turkey, Russia, and Poland* and *Incidents of Travel in Egypt, Arabia Petraea, and the Holy Land.*

Stephens' experiences abroad converted the obscure young lawyer into one of the best-known travelers and writers in America. Furthermore, they planted in him a lasting enthusiasm for monuments, ruins, and relics pertaining to antiquity. His preoccupation with the remains of ancient civilizations led him to wonder if the Western Hemisphere might somewhere conceal its own remains of civilizations that had flourished before the coming of the white man.

Simple as the idea may seem today, it was one that appeared as unlikely to most of his contemporaries as the prospect of discovering a civilization existing on the moon.

Monumental ruins of mysterious stone edifices were reported to have been seen in the jungles of Honduras, Guatemala, and Mexico. Most of the scanty literature on the subject was the work of Latin American authors. The rest was by two or three European travelers who speculated on the possibility of the crumbling structures being, somehow, the work of ancient Egyptians. Their reports placed the mysterious Central American sites at places Stephens found difficult to locate on a map. But if they really existed it seemed to him that they must have been left by a native American people whose history had been completely overlooked. He made up his mind to investigate for himself.

John Lloyd Stephens' boundless curiosity about places and the people who lived and had lived in them was shared by a friend, the English draftsman and architect Frederick Catherwood. After seeing and painting a good deal of the world, Catherwood had migrated to New York and opened an office. No business, however, not even his own, was pressing enough to keep him from accepting an invitation to go in search of an unknown chapter of history.

The two explorers sailed south by ship and then proceeded overland on horses and mules through the

jungles of Honduras. The country was as lawless as it was rugged. The deeper they invaded it, the dimmer became their hopes of finding any signs of civilization, past or present. But on reaching their destination they were rewarded beyond their most optimistic dreams. In the valley of Copán lofty stone walls rose from the tangled undergrowth. Carved stone monuments covered with marvelously ornate designs and hieroglyphs gave eloquent evidence that this country had once been occupied by people who were not uncivilized savages.

The only clues to the identity of the forgotten builders were sculptured portraits showing a strong resemblance to the faces of the Mayan Indians who were the native inhabitants of the region. Stephens observed and questioned the Indians, but all he learned was that memory or knowledge of their accomplished ancestors was as nonexistent as curiosity regarding the remains of the crumbling temples.

The drawings made by Catherwood of the ruins were so detailed and clear that they were unsurpassed by any photographic pictures being produced by the newly invented daguerreotype process. They rival, for that matter, any photographs taken of the same subject in the succeeding century.

The two explorers spent the better part of an adventurous year in the wilds of Central America. Their travels took them to the sites of three of the most spectacular Mayan ruins in existence. After rediscovering and investigating Copán they visited the lofty stone remains of Palenque, greatest of the ancient Indian cities in the state of Chiapas, Mexico. They then went to Uxmal, located in Yucatán. Stephens led the way while Catherwood, although stricken by fever, continued to make his beautiful and meticulous drawings of tumbled pyramids, temples, and palaces. At last, however, the English artist became too sick to keep on any longer. If his life were to be saved, it was imperative that he return as soon as possible to a temperate climate. Attended by Stephens, he was put aboard ship and the travelers sailed back to New York.

Soon another book by John Lloyd Stephens was selling so briskly that twelve editions were printed in three months. This one was called *Incidents of Travel in Central America,* and was strikingly illustrated with engravings from Catherwood's drawings. Before its appearance the subject of Central American archaeology had been so obscure that it was practically nonexistent. Now it was being speculated upon and discussed by thousands of readers in Europe as well as America.

Stephens led a second archaeological expedition to Central America and wrote a final Incidents of Travel, this one called *Incidents of Travel in Yucatán.* His career, however, was ended by a tragically early death from the effects of fever contracted in the tropical jungles. When he was gone, the fame and wonder of his discoveries gradually faded from the public memory.

For forty years vines and trees continued to overgrow the neglected ruins in Honduras, Guatemala, and Mexico. And then a thirty-year-old Englishman, reading *Incidents of Travel in Central America* and finding it as delightfully instructive as had numerous readers of a former generation, decided that he must see for himself these neglected remains of pre-Columbian architecture.

The reader's name was Alfred Percival Maudslay. Ten years before he had been a medical student at Cambridge. But English winters played havoc with his spirits and his health. Dreaming of a tropical climate, he had traded the prospects of a medical career for service as a colonial official. He had occupied a succession of posts in the South Pacific, first as private secretary to William Cairns, governor of Australia, and then as consul in Fiji, Samoa, and Tonga. He was back in England after filling his term overseas when he first read Stephens and was inspired to follow in the American explorer's footsteps.

Maudslay originally went to Central America as a tourist. He had no intention of studying the archaeology of the region. "However," he was to write later, in the preface to *Biologie Centrali-Americana, or Contributions to the Knowledge of the Fauna and Flora of Mexico and Central America,* "the interest awakened by the sight of the truly wonderful monuments which it was my good fortune to behold induced me to undertake other and better equipped expeditions."

He made seven other expeditions in the next thirteen years. The first two may have been no more than visits of curiosity, but the third was a full-scale archaeological campaign. With a party of assistants and workmen he spent the winter dry season of 1883 at Quiriguá, north of Copán, clearing the thick undergrowth from the ruins, taking measurements and photographs, and making paper molds and plaster casts from the monuments and inscriptions.

In successive seasons similar work was carried out at Copán, Chichén Itzá, Palenque, Tikal, and other sites which have since become famous for their ruins of pre-Columbian structures. The results of these expeditions, published in four volumes between 1889 and 1907 (*Biologie Centrali-Americana*), added to the historic record a wealth of new evidence of a native American civilization which, a thousand years before Europeans suspected the existence of America, erected stone temples atop towering pyramids, produced a powerful art in the form of carved stone sculpture, and created a system of hieroglyphic writing.

At the cost of years of effort and thousands of pounds in expense, Maudslay brought back to England a large collection of monuments, inscriptions, and facsimile copies. It was ironic that these objects and artifacts which had for centuries been hidden in remote jungles were buried again in the cellars of the Victoria and Albert Museum in London and remained there for three decades, to all practical purposes as neglected as they had been before they were discovered. But Maudslay lived to be eighty-one, and before he died he had the satisfaction of seeing his collection restored to rightful prominence and the work he had begun carried on by others who recognized him as the true founder of Central American archaeology.

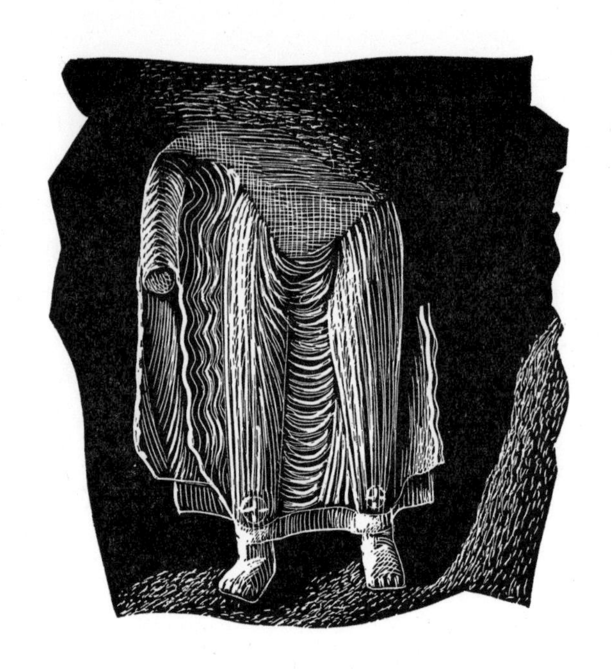

11. Travels in Desert Cathay

WHILE THE STORY of man's past was enriched by archaeological research in those familiar parts of the world where ancient civilization first appeared, increasing numbers of archaeologists, like Alfred Maudslay, were attracted to remote regions which modern civilization and historians had neglected.

On the opposite side of the globe from Central America are the desolate deserts and mountains of Central Asia. Sparsely inhabited and little traveled in modern times, the region was once criss-crossed by thriving trade routes between India and China and inhabited by people in whose culture were blended the philosophy, the literature, and the art of East and West.

Long before he had ever set foot outside his native Hungary, a young student named Mark Aurel Stein began to dream and think about the mysterious, little-known lands of Central Asia. As he continued his studies at Budapest, Dresden, Vienna, Oxford, and London he specialized in Asiatic languages and history and clung to the conviction that someday he would go to the East and explore the remains of its ancient and neglected past.

After completing his education in England he became a naturalized English subject. He secured a civil service appointment to India, where he went to serve as principal of the Oriental College at Lahore and registrar of the Punjab University. In his spare time he visited and investigated sites of archaeological interest in India. But his curiosity concerning the Asiatic lands beyond the Himalayas never diminished. Occasionally it was fed by reports of ruins and relics seen by returning travelers. In 1897 he saw a number of very old manuscripts which had been found near Khotan in the desolate Takla Makan Desert of Chinese Turkestan. These documents, consisting for the most part of Buddhist writings in archaic Indian and Chinese scripts, gave exact direction to Stein's long-standing ambition. He applied to the Indian government for support in investigating the site from which the manuscripts had come. His petition met with delays and setbacks, but at last it was granted. In 1900 he was sent on a tour of inspection to Khotan.

The Karakoram Mountains of Kashmir and Tibet are among the highest in the world. Even in summer the cloud-piercing peaks are snowcapped and blizzards howl through the passes. Aurel Stein's companions on his journey across this formidable range were two Indian assistants assigned to him by the Archaeological Survey of India, a number of servants and bearers, ponies to carry equipment and supplies, and an intrepid little fox terrier named Dash.

Stein, in addition to being an archaeologist, was a photographer and geographer. He took many fine photographs and made topographical surveys of the high, unmapped terrain over which his caravan made its way. In places the going was so rough that the baggage had to be transferred from the ponies to the backs of coolies, and on the descent into Chinese Turkestan sure-footed, slow-moving yaks were used for transport.

Once the mountains were crossed, the party rested and refitted for desert travel. Camels were hired and

water tanks made. As the hardy little explorer led his expedition across the desolate sand wastes of the Takla Makan Desert, his only fear was that nothing would be found in this vast emptiness to warrant the trust the government of India had placed in him or the expenditure of funds put at his disposal.

But his fears turned out to be unnecessary. A bitterly cold desert winter devoted to exploring and digging led to a wealth of finds which included the remains of ancient dwelling places and Buddhist shrines and temples, colorful frescoes and statuary, and hundreds of manuscripts written on paper, leather, and wood.

Ruins and relics of former habitation indicated that the desert communities of this wasteland had not always been off the traveled highways. Hundreds of years ago, before the rivers shifted their courses, grass, crops, and orchards grew in the oases. Since the last centuries before Christ and up until the eighth and ninth centuries A.D., the thriving towns were way-places along the main overland trade route connecting East and West.

From Chinese Turkestan Aurel Stein returned to London with his valuable collections of manuscripts and art objects. He was later to write of this expedition in *Ruins of Desert Cathay:* "My experiences in 1900–1901 at ruined sites in the Taklamaken Desert around

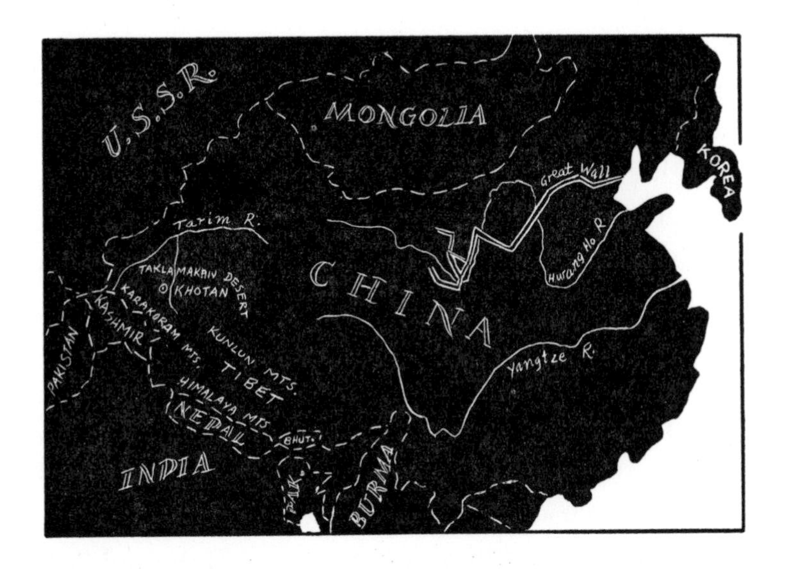

Khotan first revealed fully the great historical interest of that ancient culture which, as the joint product of Indian, Chinese, and classical influences, once flourished in the oases of Chinese Turkestan."

After the success of this journey it was not difficult to get backing for another. The government of India was taking a new and lively interest in matters of archaeology. By request of Lord Curzon, the recently appointed viceroy of India, an enterprising young English scholar named John Hubert Marshall had been installed as the director-general of the Archaeological Survey. Aurel Stein was made a part-time employee of this official government department. Under the joint auspices of the Survey and the British Museum he returned across the mountains to Chinese Turkestan. Following the track traveled by Marco Polo in the thirteenth century, he covered a vastly larger area than he had on his previous expedition. He explored a neglected section of the Great Wall of China that dated back to the second century B.C. It had been built to guard the westernmost reaches of the Chinese Empire from the Huns. In its guardhouses were found documents, equipment, and clothing that made it possible to reconstruct a picture of life along this desolate border as it had been led for many hundreds of years.

The most sensational find was an ancient Buddhist

chapel filled with perfectly preserved ninth-century religious manuscripts. Stein sent twenty-four cases of these documents, and five of ancient paintings, to the British Museum. The writings proved immensely valuable to students of oriental languages, history, and philosophy, while the paintings threw new light on the early history of Far Eastern art.

In addition to archaeological research, Stein continually made topographical surveys of the country through which he traveled, the results of which were hundreds of maps of previously uncharted terrain.

The scientific achievements of years of adventurous hard living and rough travel were not without their price in privations and hardships. Winter temperatures on the desert drop below zero at night. During summer the same region gets so hot that it becomes uninhabitable. Conditions in the high mountains are no easier. Before the explorations of 1908 were completed Stein suffered the painful experience of losing the toes of his right foot while crossing the Kunlun Mountains of Tibet at an elevation of 20,000 feet.

Aurel Stein was a bold seeker and finder who, in his lifelong attempt to extend the study of man's past into little-known areas, allowed few obstacles to bar his way. Tough and resolute, he preferred life and work in the wild deserts and mountains to the comforts of civilization. In the introduction to *Innermost Asia,* the book containing the account of his third Central Asian expedition, made from 1913 to 1916, he wrote: "While I have been engaged in the labours now completed, my thoughts have ever turned longingly to those far-off deserts and mountains which have seen the most cherished portion of my life's work. . . . Whether Fate will allow me to visit regions of innermost Asia still calling for fresh explorations, only the future can show."

Fate did allow him many rewarding years of further exploration in that rugged part of the world that comprised his chosen field of operations. He continued his strenuous travels until he was over eighty and died while on an expedition, making fresh explorations in Afghanistan.

12. Director-General of the Archaeological Survey

THE GREAT SUBCONTINENT of India occupies an area as large as all of western Europe. Its complex and colorful cultures are old. Some are as old as those of Mesopotamia, although not so long ago India was generally believed to be a relatively young country so far as its civilization was concerned.

Aurel Stein lived most of his adult life in India. Between his expeditions to other places he did a great deal of work there, studying the relationship of India's past cultures to those of Asia. It was, however, the career of Stein's colleague, John Hubert Marshall, which led to the uncovering of India's oldest civilization.

John Marshall arrived in India, a shyly confident young archaeologist with a new bride at his side, in 1902. He was a classical scholar, not long out of college. Brimming with enthusiasm for all things Greek, he had gone from Cambridge University to the British School at Athens. He had taken part in the excavations at Knossos and other sites on Crete. From Greece he was summoned to India by a telegram from Lord Curzon, the recently appointed viceroy, appointing him director-general of the Archaeological Survey.

The Survey, founded forty years earlier as a temporary government office with the function of cataloguing India's ancient monuments, was depleted in funds and personnel and its work was almost at a standstill when Lord Curzon took office. His appointment of young Dr. Marshall brought new life and a permanent status to India's official archaeological effort.

Writing many years later about the job that confronted him, Marshall said: "The task awaiting me on my arrival in India was a sufficiently formidable one. Lord Curzon's ideas of what had to be done were all-embracing. Our most pressing duty was to attend to the preservation of the national monuments, most of which were in a grievous state of neglect and decay; but the Viceroy attached almost equal importance to the exploration and study of all classes of ancient remains, to the excavation of buried sites, to the copying and reading of inscriptions and to the provision and adequate equipment of museums."

Before anything else could be done, the staff had to be enlarged. Among the new employees Marshall added to the Department, as noted earlier, was Aurel Stein, who, on a part-time basis, undertook to serve in the capacity of archaeological superintendent and inspector-general of education.

One of the principal reasons Marshall had been appointed director of the Survey was so that he might bring to India the scientific methods of excavation he had learned in Greece. He began the training of his staff during the uncovering of a number of Buddhist monasteries. These being sites about which previous knowledge already existed, the trainees were able to check the accuracy of their findings and deductions. While they were learning the precise methods of scientific archaeology, they uncovered many magnificent sculptures, fine frescoes, inscriptions, documents, and other beautiful and valuable antiquities. These discoveries did much to stimulate local interest in archaeology and inspire confidence in the Survey's work.

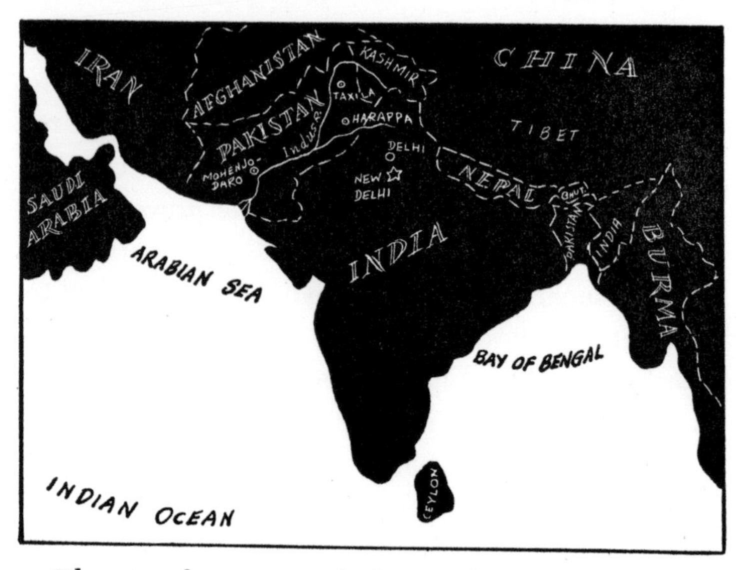

The site, however, which Marshall felt personally most drawn to was that of the ruined city of Taxila, situated on the borders of the Punjab and the northwest frontier between the Jhelum and the Indus rivers. The rocky countryside, the groves of wild olives, and the pine-covered hills reminded the young archaeologist of Greece. This city that once had stood at the junction of three ancient trade routes held strong Greek associations. History records that Alexander the Great halted there to rest his army, and Greek kings made it their capital for a hundred years thereafter.

The frontier location of the site and the lawlessness of the country made the government reluctant to give permission to dig. It was not until 1913 that Marshall could begin excavation. From then on the work continued every spring and autumn for twenty-two years.

Between 600 B.C. and A.D. 450 Taxila had been many times destroyed and rebuilt by invaders from both the East and the West. Rebuilding had not always been done on the old foundations and the ruins spread out over an area of twelve square miles. Archaeological research carried out under Marshall's direction revealed that during its thousand years of greatness Taxila was a center of commerce and learning. Study of its remains threw new light on the history of northwestern India. But the ruins of Taxila gave no indication that an earlier civilization had flourished and died out long before the first city had occupied this site.

It was at a place called Harappa, located on the banks of the Ravi in Punjab, three hundred miles from Delhi, that the first clues to the great antiquity of prehistoric Indian culture were found. For decades the rubble mounds of the ancient town had been used as brick quarries. In 1873 the first director-general of the Archaeological Survey, Sir Alexander Cunningham, had made some small excavations at Harappa. He found pottery and a polished stone engraved with pictographic writing. He knew that these objects were ancient but had no idea of their date. No further investigation of the site was made until 1921, when Daya Ram Sahni, an Indian archaeologist on Marshall's staff, dug into the rubble. The evidence he uncovered strongly indicated that the remains were a great deal older than anyone had previously suspected.

The ruins were in such bad condition, owing to age and vandalism, that Marshall hoped it would be possible to find remains of the same culture at another site. His hope was soon fulfilled. An Indian member of the Survey, R. D. Banerji, digging at Mohenjo-Daro—"the place of the dead"—about four hundred miles southwest of Harappa near the Indus River, found that the two places had once been centers of the same civilization.

Excavation uncovered the ruins of two large, highly developed cities with wide streets, closely built houses, and elaborate drainage systems. Seals bearing a pictographic form of writing were found and by their square or rectangular shapes it was possible to relate them to seals found in Mesopotamia that now could be identified as Harappan. It was possible that there had been some communication between the two countries. From this relationship with a place of known date, the approximate date of the Indus River civilization could be determined. Its beginnings went back to 2300 B.C. By 1400 B.C., when invaders from the north descended on Harappa and Mohenjo-Daro, the civilization had mostly disappeared. However, Mortimer Wheeler, the British archaeologist, believed that the civilization had still been flourishing when the invasion from the north brought the history of the two cities to a violent end.

Living and working for the major part of his professional life in India, Dr. Marshall was somewhat cut off from such improved methods of field technique as Flinders Petrie was developing in Egypt and teaching in England. His excavations consequently left room for improvement and reinterpretation. Nonetheless he opened up a completely unsuspected vista of ancient history and established India as one of the cradles of early civilization. In addition to this great discovery, he did a service to the world by directing the preservation and repair of India's decaying monuments, and an even greater service to India in particular by teaching Indians how to be their own archaeologists.

As Sir John Marshall, one of the most famous living archaeologists, he retired from the Archaeological Survey in 1929. He continued his archaeological work in India, however, for several more years. When, in 1934, he returned to England to remain there for the rest of his life, he left behind him a country that was three thousand years older than it had been when first he came to it.

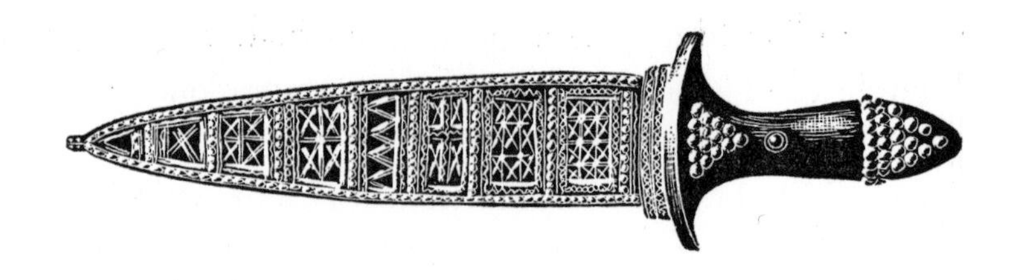

13. The Man Who Brought Dead Towns to Life

AT TEN O'CLOCK on a spring morning in 1904 an undergraduate of New College, Oxford, answered a call to appear before the Warden, or head of the college.

"Ah, Mr. Woolley," began the Warden. "Quite so. I think that when you came up to Oxford you had every intention of taking Holy Orders?"

Young Mr. Woolley murmured something unintelligible and waited.

"And now you have quite abandoned the idea."

"Oh, rather. Yes, quite, Mr. Warden, quite given it up."

"And what do you propose to do?"

"Well, I want to be a schoolmaster. I've done a little at odd times and like it awfully, so I think of going in for it permanently."

"Oh, yes, a schoolmaster, really. Well, Mr. Woolley, I have decided that you shall be an archaeologist."

And so, as he was to report later in his autobiography, *Dead Towns and Living Men,* Charles Leonard Woolley found a career. His actual preparation took place in the Ashmolean Museum of Art and Archaeology at Oxford, where he served as an assistant under Arthur Evans, and then in Egypt where he learned to dig without damaging what the ground contained, to use knife and brush for unearthing delicate objects, and to manage native workmen and deal with local bureaucrats.

He found ample opportunity to demonstrate how well he had learned to handle people in order to reach his goals, when he went from Egypt to Turkish-ruled Syria in 1912 to excavate the ancient Hittite capital of Carchemish. As soon as he arrived he hired workmen. Then he learned that the Turkish governor refused to give permission to excavate, in spite of the fact that official arrangements had already been completed with the higher authorities at Constantinople. A detail of

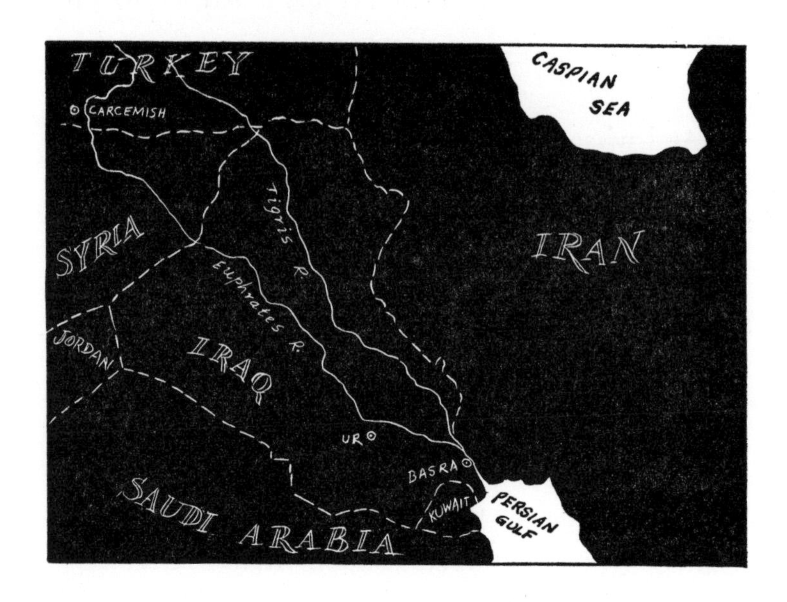

soldiers was standing guard at the excavation site to enforce the governor's orders.

Woolley was accompanied by T. E. Lawrence—later to become famous as "Lawrence of Arabia," a leader of the Arabs in their uprising against the Turks, but then a young archaeologist only a year or two out of Oxford. They mounted their horses and rode twenty-five miles to the provincial government center. There the governor refused to see them, but they entered his office uninvited and attempted to reason with him. When all words failed, Woolley drew his revolver and placed the muzzle against the Turk's head. Further discussion proved unnecessary. A permit was promptly drawn up allowing work to begin next day.

The remains of ancient Carchemish lay buried beneath layer upon layer of rubble of successive towns built on the same site. Beneath the Byzantine ruins of early Christian times lay the Roman, beneath the Roman the Greek, and lastly, under everything, the relics of the great days of the Hittites.

Scholars knew, by references to them in the Bible and in Egyptian and Assyrian texts, that the Hittites had been one of the principal powers of the ancient world. But material evidence had eluded the archaeologists until, in 1879, a British orientalist named Archibald Henry Sayce advanced the theory that certain unidentified ruins which travelers had reported seeing in Asia Minor and northern Syria were of Hittite origin. In 1906 and 1907 a German expedition under Dr. Hugo Winkler dug at Bogazköy in Turkey and found a fortified Hittite city and thousands of inscribed clay tablets. A few years later the British Museum sent to Carchemish the expedition with which Woolley was associated.

In 1919, after time out from archaeology to serve as an intelligence officer with the British army, Woolley was back at Carchemish, the city that ". . . went down in smoke and tumult two thousand five hundred years ago." In *Dead Towns and Living Men* (Philosophical Library) he describes it as it is and as it was: ". . . about you and above are the long rows of sculptured figures, gods and beasts and fighting men, and inscriptions in honour of forgotten kings; statues of old deities; wide stairways and gates, where the ashes of the doors still lie in the corners of the threshold; column-bases whose shafts were of cedar and their capitals of bronze wrought in patterns of nets and pomegranates—and the scarlet anemones push up between the stones, and the lizards sun themselves on the walls of palace or temple, and the spring wind drives the dust over the ruins of the imperial city. Very magnificent must Carchemish have been when its sculptures were gay with colour, when the sunlight glistened on its enamelled walls, and its sombre brick was overlaid with panels of cedar and plates of bronze; when the plumed horses rattled their chariots along its streets, and the great lords, with long embroidered robes and girdles of black and gold, passed in and out of the carved gates of its palaces; . . . ."

When unsettled political conditions in Syria made it impossible to go on with the work at Carchemish, the British Museum appointed Woolley director of an expedition which, under the joint sponsorship of that institution and the University Museum of Pennsyl-

vania, went to southern Mesopotamia to uncover the ancient Sumerian city of Ur.

The ruins had first been excavated by J. E. Taylor, British Consul at Basra, in 1854. He found inscriptions identifying the site as Ur of the Chaldees, the biblical home of Abraham. He dug during two seasons, but the wild and lawless character of the region discouraged further investigation for forty years. Toward the end of the nineteenth century the University Museum of Pennsylvania sent its first expedition to Ur. The results were never published. It was not until World War I brought British troops to Mesopotamia that interest in the site revived.

Splendid though Hittite Carchemish had been, and ancient as it is, Ur was even older and more splendid. The site it occupied was so immense that in twelve consecutive seasons only a portion of it could be uncovered and studied. That portion, however, revealed the remains of a capital founded and long inhabited by the earliest civilized people in the world.

In *History Unearthed* Woolley wrote: "The most important result obtained from the excavations at Ur was that the dated history of Mesopotamia was carried back for half a millennium and the culture of a period hitherto quite unknown was illustrated by the astonishing richness of the royal tombs."

The tombs were discovered below a layer of remains known to date to the time of the first king of the First Dynasty of Ur. This ancient cemetery contained the tombs of sixteen kings and queens and the graves of hundreds of their subjects. From the archaeological evidence it was apparent that the retinue of each ruler had gone with him to the grave. Women dressed in their finery and jewels, officers with their arms, and musicians with their instruments, all had been victims of a custom which demanded that they be buried with their deceased monarchs.

The discovery of the royal tombs was not only a high spot in Leonard Woolley's career, but it was also one of the most sensational finds in the history of archaeology. Like Schliemann's unearthing of Troy and Carter's opening of King Tutankhamen's tomb, it attracted the attention and aroused the wonder of the public all over the world.

The essential business of an archaeologist's life, however, is not finding treasure so much as it is finding and interpreting factual evidence. After the close of the combined British Museum and University Museum of Pennsylvania campaign, Woolley went to India to inspect the Archaeological Survey and make recommendations for its reorganization. In 1936 he returned to northern Syria where he spent a number of profitable seasons excavating on the Amuq plain, between the Mediterranean and the valley of the Tigris and Euphrates rivers. Here he found remains of human habitation going back five thousand years and more. Babylon and Egypt had left their marks on the region. In the customs and tastes of its early inhabitants could be discerned roots of the Aegean civilization which Evans unearthed at Knossos and Schliemann at Mycenae.

For his painstaking work on the farthermost frontiers of ancient history and prehistory, Woolley's name seldom appeared in the newspaper headlines, as it had when he was uncovering the royal tombs of Ur but he was recognized everywhere in the world of scholarship as one of the greatest field archaeologists ever to dig a trench. With his spadework and his poetic gift for self-expression, he could make the dead towns he unearthed live again in the minds of men. He continued to advance the science of archaeology and to throw new light on old civilizations until only recently. The last years of his life were spent in England, where he died in February, 1960, at the age of seventy-nine.

14. Still Digging

WHEN LEONARD WOOLLEY visited India to inspect the Archaeological Survey and its work, it had been nearly ten years since John Marshall's retirement as director-general. The Survey was suffering from lack of leadership and want of funds. Woolley's suggestions for reorganization included the return to India of a European adviser in archaeology. He recommended British archaeologist Mortimer Wheeler as the best man for the job.

Robert Eric Mortimer Wheeler was Woolley's junior by about twenty years. He had received his formal education at London University. There, as an undergraduate back in the days before World War I, he had often cut his classes in order to take instruction in painting at the Slade School of Fine Arts. But his youthful ardor to be a painter was gradually cooled by the realization that should he become one he would have to be an innovator and starve or else a conventionally accomplished picture-maker and earn a living. One alternative being as undesirable as the other, he forsook the practice of art and decided to be an archaeologist.

A part-time job in the office of the university provost enabled him to go on to graduate study after receiving his bachelor's degree. When a scholarship in archaeology, offering £50 a year, became available he had to make a decision between applying for it or holding onto the somewhat shaky security of his £120-a-year job. He applied for the scholarship and got it.

One of the members of the imposing committee which examined him was Sir Arthur Evans. As the student walked thoughtfully from the examining room he heard footsteps in the corridor behind him. He turned to find himself face to face with Sir Arthur.

"That £50," the excavator of Knossos said quietly. "It isn't much. I should like to double it for you."

And so, in 1913, backed by the generous support of one of the foremost archaeologists in the world, Mortimer Wheeler set out on his career. Only a year later, however, the outbreak of World War I converted the budding scientist into a Royal Artillery officer. Not until the armistice in 1919, by which time he was twenty-nine years old, with a wife and son to support, was he able to settle down in earnest to the practice of his profession.

The maturity a man gains in war sometimes helps to compensate for the time lost from his chosen work. It was maturity, and a sense of fleeting time, and perhaps hard-won respect for the discipline of military thinking, that made Wheeler, in starting afresh, adopt for his model the strictest of old-school perfectionists. He resolved to set his sights on the high standards established by General Pitt-Rivers.

After the war he returned to a job as junior investigator under the Royal Commission on Historical Monuments which he had held for a short time. The work, consisting of cataloguing the contents of old churches and manor houses, was hardly lucrative and held little promise for the future. The National Museum of Wales was advertising for a Keeper of Archaeology. Wheeler applied and was hired.

The museum was an impoverished institution without an edifice to house its collection or a public to view it. Dr. Wheeler aroused popular interest in archaeology by lecturing throughout Wales and excavating ancient Roman sites. Under his administration the museum's debt was wiped out, a new building was completed and paid for, and the King of England came to officiate at the opening ceremonies.

From Wales Wheeler went to London. As director of the London Museum he repeated the performance of revitalizing a neglected institution. With help from Flinders Petrie he also made plans for the founding of a school where archaeologists of the future could learn the basic essentials of their exacting business. To be known as the Institute of Archaeology, it would be a new department of his own alma mater, London University.

In addition to administrative duties, fund raising, and lecturing, he continued to apply his high standards of technique to uncovering the remains of prehistoric and Roman Britain. In the 1930s, helped by his wife and many of his students, he excavated the prehistoric fortification called Maiden Castle. The ancient earthworks, near Dorchester in southern England, had been likened by the novelist Thomas Hardy to an ". . . enormous many limbed organism of an antediluvian time . . . lying lifeless, and covered with a thin green cloth, which hides its substance, while revealing its contour."

Scattered finds of pottery and coins indicated that the ruins were Roman in origin. But they had never been scientifically studied. Dr. Wheeler, directing the excavation with such thoroughness that General Pitt-Rivers could not but have approved, uncovered a story of human habitation that began in the Stone Age, nearly two thousand years before the coming of the conquering Roman legions.

In preparation for his forthcoming duties as the first director of the Institute of Archaeology, Dr. Wheeler interrupted his work at Maiden Castle in the spring of 1936 to go to the Middle East and acquaint himself with what was being done at the many sites being excavated by archaeological expeditions from several nations. He was astonished at the technical sloppiness of much of the work. In his autobiography, *Still Digging*, he was to write ". . . from the Sinai border to Megiddo and on to Byblos and northern Syria, I encountered such technical standards as had not been tolerated in Great Britain for a quarter of a century."

While he was gone his wife was taken suddenly ill. She died before he could get back to her. With a heavy heart he recalled the last time he had seen her. As he had left for his trip she was standing in the doorway of their London apartment and calling quietly down the stairs to him, "Goodbye—and remember, you are very precious."

He combated the bitter sense of loss with incessant application to his work. There was the Institute of Archaeology, for which he had labored so long and arduously. With its formal opening in 1937 was initiated a means for improving the standards he had found so disappointing in the Middle East. There was his schedule of teaching and lecturing, and there was his busy program of work in the field.

After four richly rewarding seasons the excavations at Maiden Castle were closed down in 1938. The findings there, and at other Roman sites in Great Britain, led to the investigation of similar sites across the English Channel in northern France.

Here Dr. Wheeler and his staff found and studied a series of Roman camps of great size which belonged to the period of Caesar's campaigns in the fifties of the first century B.C.

The portents of World War II brought an end to archaeological research in France. Returning home, Wheeler once again changed his academic title for a military one. He fought with the 8th Army in Africa and rose to be the commander of a brigade. During the brief respites he was allowed from war he made an

archaeological reconnaissance of Roman ruins on the Libyan coast, and the previously mentioned visit to Flinders Petrie on his deathbed in Palestine.

While he was in Africa a message came to Brigadier Wheeler from India. It was an invitation to take over the post of director-general of the Archaeological Survey. It arrived at the time when the Allies were planning the invasion of Italy. Not wanting to leave the job he was involved in until it was completed, Wheeler replied that he would be willing to accept if, in six months, his service was still required.

As commanding officer of the 12th Anti-Aircraft Brigade he participated in the allied landings at Salerno.

Not until Italy surrendered was he ready to return to civilian responsibilities. Then, the offer from India still open, he took off his uniform for the last time and embarked for his new post.

The newly appointed director-general, direct from the battlefield, alerted the lagging Archaeological Survey with a resounding reveille. He reorganized the administrative staff and opened a training school for field work at Taxila. Under his direction excavation was resumed at Harappa and Mohenjo-Daro, where new discoveries led to revised interpretation of the Indus River civilization. On his first visit to southern India his experienced eye recognized the remains of former Roman colonization. He revised publication of archaeological reports and, with his usual flair for public relations, did everything he could to reawaken the interest of Indians in their country's past.

In restoring the Survey to its former status the director-general introduced to India the administrative genius which had founded the Institute of Archaeology of London University and the high standards of technique which he had developed from the earlier techniques of Flinders Petrie and General Pitt-Rivers.

After the independence and partition of India Dr. Wheeler was invited to Pakistan as a part-time archaeological adviser. From 1948 to 1950 he spent three or four months each year in Pakistan and the rest of his time at the University of London.

Knighted in 1952, he retired from his professorship three years later. Since that time he has devoted part of his tremendous energy to making films for the British Broadcasting Company in Africa, India, and Pakistan. Today, in keeping with his lifelong policy of bringing scientific knowledge and archaeological awareness to the public, Sir Mortimer Wheeler is known to millions not only as an outstanding scientist but also as one of Great Britain's most popular TV and radio personalities.

15. The Mystery of Linear B

AT THE AGE OF SIX, when many children are learning to spell c-a-t, a precocious English boy astonished his mother and father by undertaking to teach himself Polish. By the time he was seven he was studying Egyptian hieroglyphics from a book written in German.

His name was Michael Ventris. Figuring out the meaning and memorizing the sounds of exotic languages was far more fun to him than the games and puzzles that amused his playmates. As he grew bigger he was sent away to school in Switzerland where the lessons were taught in French and German and he learned to speak the local German-Swiss dialect like a native.

One day in 1936, when Michael was fourteen, he happened to be taken to a lecture in London delivered by Sir Arthur Evans, who was then eighty-five. The grand old man of Greek archaeology, mentor of Leonard Woolley and Mortimer Wheeler, told how his discovery of hieroglyphic-like markings on tiny seals from Mycenae and Crete had given him cause to wonder if the ancient inhabitants of those places had known how to write. He described the unearthing of the long-forgotten civilization of Crete and the treasures that were uncovered at Knossos, including many inscribed seals and tablets.

In the years since the inscriptions were discovered neither Arthur Evans nor anyone else had learned to read them, or even to recognize what language they represented. As a matter of fact, they were apparently in two languages, one even older than the other. Their discoverer had labeled the older script Linear A and the other, more prevalent one, he called Linear B.

For a boy who was fascinated by strange languages, the mystery of the Minoan script was a never-to-be-forgotten challenge. How much thought Michael Ventris must have given it is apparent from the fact that four years after hearing Evans lecture he wrote an article, entitled "Introducing the Minoan Language," which was published in the *American Journal of Archaeology*. In it he ventured the opinion that if Linear B could be deciphered it would prove to be Etruscan.

It was only a theory. Few scholars were willing to accept it, but at the same time none had anything better to offer. The one point on which most of them agreed was that it could *not* be Greek because the Greek language had not yet come into existence at such an early date.

Keenly interested though he was in deciphering Linear B, there were other activities and problems demanding Michael Ventris' attention. There was his education. He was preparing to be an architect. The war interrupted his schooling. He joined the Royal Air Force and became a navigator. After the war he returned to his studies and took his degree. He married and began to practice his new profession.

But all the while he was haunted by the unsolved mystery of the language of ancient Crete and Mycenae. He continued to study it, memorizing all the characters, comparing them, attempting to analyze their variations. As he got further and further into the subject he corresponded and compared notes with others who were working on the same problem. One of these was an American scholar named Dr. Alice E. Kober. She arrived at a number of partial solutions to the structure of the language, but her brilliant work came to a premature end when she died in 1950 at the age of forty-three.

In the same year Ventris wrote a progress report setting forth what had been accomplished to date by himself and those with whom he had been in correspondence. In concluding the report he stated: "I have good hopes that a sufficient number of people working on these lines will before long enable a satisfactory solution to be found. To them I offer my best wishes, being forced by pressure of other work to make this my last small contribution to the problem."

The subject, however, was not to be so easily dismissed. During the next two years he not only found time to go on with his study of Linear B but mastered it to such an extent that in June, 1952, he was able to make a historic announcement. In the course of a talk on the Minoan script, delivered over the British Broadcasting Company radio, he told that many of the Minoan and Mycenaean documents were beginning to make sense. The language in which they were written was Greek; "—a difficult and archaic Greek, seeing that it is five hundred years older than Homer and written in a rather abbreviated form, but Greek nevertheless."

Announcement of a discovery that does not conform to previous ideas often meets with strong opposition. But so thoroughly had Ventris done his work that most scholars were both gracious and grateful in their acceptance of his solution. Professor Martin Nilsson, Swedish authority on Greek and Mycenaean religion, pointed out that Ventris' achievement in deciphering Linear B was greater than Champollion's in deciphering the Egyptian hieroglyphs. Champollion had the help of the Rosetta stone, with its parallel text in a

known language, whereas Ventris had opened the door without a key.

Combinations of signs appeared on tablets and by studying them he was able to identify certain words and even to place them as nouns, verbs, or conjunctions. Nouns, for instance, could be located from some tablets which seemed to be lists of things. Ventris found a sequence of number signs; these stood for the quantities of some items. He studied word endings, particularly of nouns, and the way they seemed to follow a grammatical structure. And he applied what he knew of the construction of other ancient languages to the problem.

Once translated, what did the records, inscribed in the earliest known written language of Europe, have to say? The tablets found at Knossos and a number of Mycenaean sites were, for the most part, business records and inventories. Some were concerned with military matters. They hardly constituted a literature but they revealed a wealth of details from the day-to-day lives of the inhabitants of these places—such as their occupations, the commodities they used and in which they traded, the structure of civil and military organizations, taxation, methods of reckoning, and various statistics.

Although Michael Ventris was not an archaeologist by profession, his solution to the mystery of Linear B was a highlight in archaeological accomplishment. It answered problems left unsolved by both Schliemann and Evans and established a new milestone in the progress of research in Aegean prehistory. There could no longer be any doubt that the Mycenaeans were Greeks. Once the fact was established, and added to the knowledge that Mycenae and Knossos used the same language, the relationship between the two could be viewed in a new light. Sir Arthur Evans had believed that Mycenae developed under the influence of Crete. It now seemed probable that Crete, in its heyday, had been strongly influenced by Mycenae.

Having led the break-through in deciphering Linear B, Ventris spent the next four years enlarging his understanding of the script, studying and translating new material discovered by archaeologists in the field, and writing about his achievement.

In September, 1956, he was killed in an automobile accident. He was only thirty-four years old. His early death was an irretrievable loss to science and humanity. He was as widely loved for his charm and modesty as he was esteemed for his brilliance. The world could ill afford to lose him. In his short life Michael Ventris played a spectacular role in the efforts of science to throw its light on the remote past.

16. The Abbé and the Painted Caves

In the vicinity of almost any small town there usually is some spot around which a legend clings—a haunted house, a deserted quarry, or a peculiar feature of the terrain.

Outside the village of Montignac, in southwestern France, it was nothing more than a hole left by an uprooted tree. The hole was not large, but there were stories that persisted about it. An old woman of Montignac claimed that it marked the entrance to a secret tunnel leading to the château which stood at the edge of town.

Nobody had ever done anything to find out whether she was right or wrong until one September day in 1940 an eighteen-year-old boy named Marcel Ravidat led three of his friends to the place with the idea of exploring it.

Marcel took a lamp with him—just in case. When they got to the hole he began to dig. Loose pebbles rolled down the side of the excavation and filtered through a small opening at the bottom. They could be heard striking some distance below with a hollow sound, like stones tossed into a dry well.

Suddenly the earth collapsed under Marcel and he plunged into a dark shaft. He landed unharmed in a pile of loose dirt. As soon as he recovered from the shock he lit his lamp and looked around. He was in a large underground vault. Beyond the circle of his light he was confronted by an empty, cavernous darkness.

He called to his companions to follow him. In silent awe the boys advanced into the cave. They had not gone far before they realized that they were not entirely alone. Around them loomed a cavalcade of animals—bulls, horses, and antlered deer—depicted on the walls in softly glowing colors.

Caves containing prehistoric paintings had been

found before in the region. In fact, southwestern France and northern Spain are noted for their ancient painted caves. The boys knew that such places were of great importance and that people came from all over the world to see them. They whooped and danced with joy, but when their outburst was over they agreed that they would tell nobody.

The secret, however, was too big to keep. They returned to the cave on several successive days to explore it. After finding that it consisted not only of the great vaulted hall into which the hole had led them but also of several long passageways and other chambers—all covered with hundreds of marvelously painted animals—they told the local schoolmaster what they had found.

The news spread rapidly. Fortunately one of the first to hear it was a man who ranked among France's, if not the world's, greatest authorities on prehistoric cave art. He was the renowned Abbé Henri Édouard Prosper Breuil.

Since boyhood Henri Breuil had been an enthusiastic student of nature. He was gifted with insatiable curiosity that compelled him to investigate the how and why of everything around him, and a keen sense of observation to help him in his quest. His first love was entomology, the study of insects, but he also studied

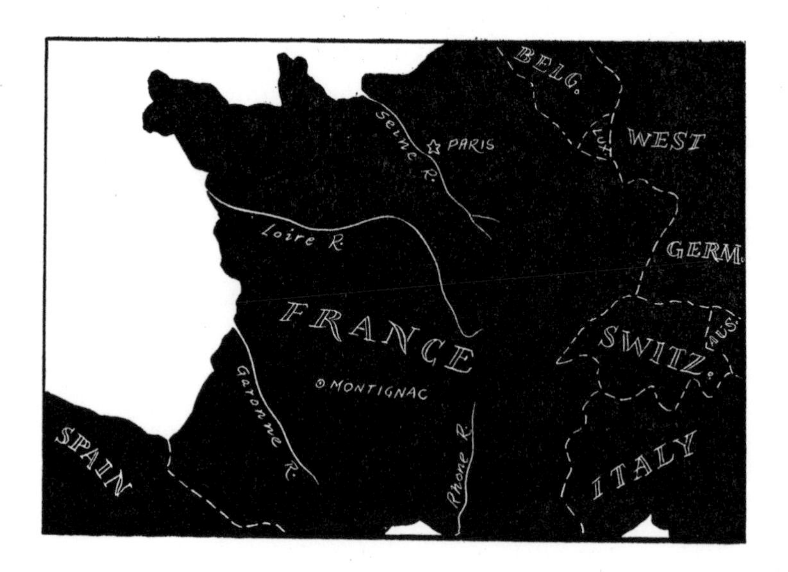

geology and liked to draw. On visits to his grandparents' farm he saw ancient stone axes and tools that had been turned up by the plow, and these things made him wonder about the people who long ago had made and used them. As he was to write many years later, in the introduction to *Beyond the Bounds of History*, one of his several books about ancient man and his art, "Humanity's long past opened before me and I began to dream."

At the age of eighteen he entered the Seminary of St. Sulpice in Paris. One of his professors, impressed by the boy's enthusiasm for science and art, encouraged him to study archaeology. Delving further and deeper into the subject, he found himself drawn back to the very earliest known period of human culture, represented by the stone tools and cave paintings of the Palaeolithic, or Old, Stone Age.

He began to spend several months every year exploring caves for evidence of bygone human activity. Where there were paintings, he studied them and made copies. Except for a few bones, worked stones, and ashes these paintings comprise the entire remaining record of the people who produced them. According to geological evidence, many were painted as long ago as twenty thousand years. Indications of human habitation were rare in the painted caves, pointing to the conclusion that they had been used only as gathering places and that the pictures were painted by priests or medicine men for magic or religious reasons—perhaps to help in the hunt for the animals depicted.

Although they tell very little about the day-to-day lives of the cave painters of the Old Stone Age these cavalcades of accurately observed and beautifully rendered animals disclose that long before mankind knew how to raise crops or build villages or indicate words by means of written symbols, he possessed the skill, the power of intellect, and the nobility of spirit to create art.

The cave discovered by Marcel Ravidat and his friends came to be called Lascaux. Upon paying his first visit to it, Abbé Breuil knew at once that this was the high point of nearly half a century of studying Palaeolithic art in France, Spain, and Africa. The paintings of Lascaux are perhaps the earliest works of art ever created, and certainly rank among the most magnificent.

The researches of the Abbé Breuil, and other palaeontologists and archaeologists of many nations, is pushing back the record of man's past achievement to its remotest limits. But the study of the past is still a young science. As far as archaeology is concerned the world is only partially explored.

To the skillful methods of excavation developed by the foremost archaeologists of the nineteenth century have been added many technological developments of the twentieth. The airplane, for example, has proved a great boon to archaeology. Not only does it shorten travel time between modern cities and ancient ruins, but also it makes possible aerial photography. Strange as it may seem, the faint ground markings that indicate places where buildings once stood are sometimes clearly visible from the air when they are invisible to a would-be observer standing right on them.

Another innovation that has enlarged the archaeologist's scope is the aqualung and the lively art of skin diving. Many relics of the past lie under water. The floor of the Mediterranean is littered with decayed wrecks of Greek and Roman galleys and the remains of their cargoes. At various places in the world the seas have encroached on the land and covered buildings and towns. By making possible the recovery of drowned relics, submarine exploration is enlarging the realm of archaeology and enriching our knowledge of the past.

The most important modern development to affect archaeology has come from the field of chemistry. It is the so-called carbon-14 dating technique, pioneered by Dr. Willard F. Libby of the United States. Carbon 14 utilizes the fact that all living organisms contain radioactive carbon, which they take into their systems from the atmosphere while they are alive. As soon as any organism dies it begins to radiate the radioactive carbon it has absorbed up to that time. The radiation dissipates at a constant rate. By determining the amount of radioactive carbon remaining in a once living object, such as a piece of bone or wood, chemists can determine how long it has been since the organism was alive. Never has archaeology had such an accurate dating method. For his part in the development of this technique, Dr. Libby was awarded the 1960 Nobel Prize in chemistry.

Every advance in archaeology is the opening of a door that presents a new vista into the past, and an improved understanding of the past. By increasing his knowledge of human achievement, mankind is better able to understand the human mind. He seeks to know who he is by finding out who he was, to learn where he is going by where he has been. But the history of mankind is a story that can never be completely told. As the future becomes the present and the present becomes the past, and the world grows older, the archaeologist's work perennially begins anew.

Notable Archaeologists

Botta (boat′-ah), *Paul Émile* (1802–1870), French explorer and archaeologist. Pioneer excavator in Mesopotamia.

Breasted (bres′-ted), *James Henry* (1865–1935), American archaeologist and orientalist. Founder of the Oriental Institute of the University of Chicago.

Breuil (bre-oy′), *Henri Édouard Prosper* (1877–), French archaeologist. One of the foremost living authorities on prehistoric cave painting.

Champollion (sham-pole-yon′), *Jean François* (1790–1832), French Egyptologist. Decipherer of the Egyptian hieroglyphics.

Denon (deh-non′), *Dominique Vivant* (1747–1825), French artist, diplomat, and archaeologist. Accompanied Napoleon to Egypt.

Evans (ev′-anz), *Arthur John* (1851–1941), British archaeologist. Excavator of Knossos and discoverer of the Minoan civilization on the island of Crete.

Lane Fox, Augustus Henry, became General Pitt-Rivers

(1827–1900), British army officer and archaeologist. One of the first scientific excavators.

Layard (lay′-ard), *Austen Henry* (1817–1894), British author and diplomat. Excavator of Nineveh in Mesopotamia.

Lepsius (lep′-see-us), *Karl Richard* (1810–1884), German philologist, archaeologist, and pioneer Egyptologist.

Mariette (ma-ree-et′), *Auguste Ferdinand François* (1821–1881), French archaeologist and pioneer Egyptologist.

Marshall (mar′-shall), *John Hubert* (1876–1959), British archaeologist. Director-general of the Archaeological Survey of India from 1902 to 1929. Excavator of the Indus River culture.

Maudslay (maud′-zlee), *Alfred Percival* (1850–1931), British traveler and archaeologist. The founder of Central American archaeology.

Petrie (pee′-tree), *William Matthew Flinders* (1853–1942), British archaeologist. Director of excavations in Egypt and Palestine. Often called the father of modern archaeology.

Schliemann (shlee′-man), *Heinrich* (1822–1890), German archaeologist. Discoverer of Troy and the Mycenaean civilization.

Stein (styne), *Mark Aurel* (1862–1943), Hungarian-born British archaeologist and explorer. Outstanding authority on the archaeology of Central Asia.

Stephens (stee′-venz), *John Lloyd* (1805–1852), American traveler, author, and archaeologist. One of the first explorers of the Mayan ruins in Central America.

Thomsen (tom′-sen), *Christian Jørgensen* (1788–1865),

Danish antiquarian and originator of the Three Age System for classifying prehistoric remains.

Ventris (ven′-triss), *Michael* (1922–1956), British architect and amateur philologist. Decipherer of the Minoan script (Linear B).

Wheeler (wheel′-er), *Robert Eric Mortimer* (1890–), one of the foremost British archaeologists living today.

Winckelmann (vin′-kel-man), *Johann Joachim* (1717–1768), German scholar, art historian, and antiquarian.

Woolley (wool′-lee), *Charles Leonard* (1880–1960), British archaeologist. Director of excavations in Syria and Mesopotamia. Excavator of Ur.

Suggestions for Further Reading

BACON, EDWARD. *Digging for History*. New York: The John Day Company, 1960. A great deal of information on what's new in archaeology.

BRAYMER, MARJORIE. *The Walls of Windy Troy*. New York: Harcourt, Brace & World, Inc., 1960. A biography of Heinrich Schliemann.

CERAM, C. W. *Gods, Graves, and Scholars*. New York: A. A. Knopf, 1952. A popular book about some of the greatest archaeologists and their discoveries.

———. *The March of Archaeology*. New York: Alfred A. Knopf, Inc., 1958. A handsomely illustrated pictorial history of archaeology.

COTTRELL, LEONARD. *Lost Cities*. New York: Rinehart & Co., Inc., 1957. A book about many of the most important archaeological discoveries and the archaeologists who made them.

———. *The Mountains of Pharaoh*. New York: Rinehart & Co., Inc., 1956. The story of archaeology in Egypt, illustrated with photographs and diagrams.

DANIEL, GLYN. *A Hundred Years of Archaeology.* London: Duckworth, 1950. An excellent all-inclusive survey of the principal events and the significant personalities in archaeology.

HONOUR, ALAN. *Secrets of Minos.* New York: Whittlesey House, 1961. A biography of Sir Arthur Evans for young adults.

JESSUP, RONALD FREDERICK. *The Wonderful World of Archaeology.* Garden City: Garden City Books, 1956. A large-size, colorfully illustrated history of archaeology for the younger reader.

WOOLLEY, SIR LEONARD. *History Unearthed.* London: Ernest Benn, Ltd., 1958. Short descriptions of eighteen important archaeological sites all over the world, illustrated with numerous photographs.

Index

ABOUT THE AUTHOR

In 1953, Charles Michael Daugherty accompanied the Inca Highway Expedition to Peru as a photographer. His experiences there provided a stimulant to his interest in archaeology. However, Mr. Daugherty's interests span many fields and he has published books on a variety of subjects.

In addition to writing, he has followed careers in the graphic arts, painting, and photography and has traveled extensively. Born in New York, and raised there and in Connecticut, Mr. Daugherty studied at the Yale University School of Fine Arts and the Art Students League. He is currently living in New York City.

ABOUT THE ILLUSTRATOR

Leonard Everett Fisher received his early training at the Art Students League, at the studio of Moses and Raphael Soyer and at the Heckscher Foundation in New York City. He received both a B.F.A. and an M.F.A. from the Yale University School of Fine Arts.

He interrupted his studies during World War II to serve in the army as a topographic editor and then as a photogrammetrist, making maps from photographs. Mr. Fisher, who has illustrated more than seventy books (and is the author of three), has served as Dean of the Whitney School of Art in New Haven, Connecticut.

Mr. Fisher, his wife, and three children live in Westport, Connecticut.